To Will

Positive Money - 7 Principles for Living a Rich Life

no matter what's in your bank account

Cindy Morgan-Jaffe

Positive Money Club

Illustrations by Rose Jaffe

Praise for Positive Money

“Cindy Morgan-Jaffe's expertise on money and relationships has been featured in national publications and is now accessible to everyone who needs this guidance on how to turn the complicated relationship we all have with money — into Positive Money.

— *Iris Krasnow, Best Selling Author and Senior Editor AARP's The Ethel*

“Most money books teach you how to get rich while Positive Money teaches you how to live richly.

— *Tammy Lally, The Money Coach and Author of Money Detox*

“Our relationship with money is an exact reflection of our deepest-held beliefs about our own worth. It relates to deeply personal and spiritual issues that go far beyond spending, earning, and debt. Through wisdom, humor, and compassion, Cindy will help you understand the complexity and beauty of money to help you change those deepest beliefs.

— Meadow DeVor, Author of The Worthy Project and Money Love

“Positive Money helps you create wealth from the inside out. Powerful principles and simple practices will help reset your money mind, reclaim your self-worth, and have better money conversations with others. This valuable book provides positive solutions to your inner money struggles so you can lead a richer life.

— Debra Jean Rogers, Book Coach and Award-Winning Author of He Did You a Favor

“Positive Money is so needed by individuals, families, and business owners as our relationship with money can be complicated and not something we talk about or deal with. I’ve known Cindy for over 20 years and appreciate her passion to help individuals learn more about themselves, heal, and grow!

— Tom Karl, Founder & CEO of R1 Learning

> Positive Money gives us an amazing system to consciously build a prosperity mindset, no matter what beliefs we inherited. Parents can learn from this to instill the same growth mindset in their kids, empowering them with a life of financial strength.
>
> — *Gayle Reaume, CEO & Founder, Moolah U*

> In a world where so much financial advice is laced with shame, guilt, and scarcity, Positive Money is exactly what we need to embrace abundance and empower ourselves to change our relationship with money for the better.
>
> — *Jamie Trull, Founder of Balance CFO*

> Cindy sheds light on the shame and blame we can carry in our relationship with money. As one of our certified recovery coaches, she brings a sensitivity to the challenges families and individuals can face around this sensitive topic and offers thoughtful and holistic solutions.
>
> — *Dr. Jean LaCour, President/CEO Int'l Center for Addiction & Recovery Education (ICARE)*

“Cindy has written an outstanding book that will help you have a richer life by changing your relationship and mindset about money using her 7 Principles. Positive Money is filled with practical exercises, stories, and coaching examples to help guide you through the journey. Regardless of your paycheck or bank statement, this book is essential reading for everyone who wants to find a better way to work with money.

— Wendy S. Swire, Executive Coach and Author of Anytime Coaching: Unleashing Employee Performance

“Positive Money is a beautiful way to change your relationship with money by creating a better relationship with yourself. Cindy's case studies and examples really help bring her 7 Principles to life in inspiring ways.

— Stephanie Klein, Executive Coach and Author

“Cindy brings a wealth of knowledge, experience, and dedication to her work as a coach, educator, and speaker about Positive Money.

— Nikki Bradley, Brand Expert

“I'm in awe of Cindy's talent to change my negative narratives into conscious, positive, goal-oriented habits that align with my head and heart.

— Susie Alexander, Artist

> Positive Money Principles have kept me calm, clear, and focused so I can be courageous as I reinvent my business to be more in line with the impact I want to generate in the world.
>
> — *Janna Jorgenson, Creator of the Human Impact Framework*

> Cindy brilliantly simplified my journey toward a healthy money mindset. After making progress with other exceptional systems, her 7 Principles are what I need to make consistent, wise choices.
>
> — *Roberta Ryan, Business Coach*

Contents

Letter to a Rich Girl

This past year, while visiting my childhood home, I found a letter my mother wrote to me when I was away at college in 1979. It was in a box of correspondence I'd saved and stashed away in a closet in my old bedroom. When I opened the letter, I noticed she'd typed it on our family stationery with her favorite electric typewriter and that she'd included her signature handwritten notes along the margins. The following is an excerpt:

Dear Cindy,

I have a favor to ask of you. Try not to say 'rich', expensive, money (with a sneer) for a whole year. Try to keep the words out of your vocabulary. My mother used to say 'nice girls NEVER refer to money or the price of things, etc.' but this is not my point. To always keep labeling people as rich means nothing and is demeaning to them. If it is a son or daughter, the situation is something they cannot help. Remember that you are a rich girl. Many people in our community feel we are the 'haves'. And it is not very pleasant when that is rubbed in as if it were a terrible disease. There are always richer or poorer people and neither wants to be reminded of that status. It has nothing to do with whether someone is a fine person, or a creative and kind human being. Those come in all sizes and shapes and with all sizes of money bags.

When you were all little, I used to call you 'little turds'... finally, Daddy pointed out what my affectionate little term means, and I never used it again. Sometimes you forget the real meaning of things."

* * *

I had no recollection of this letter, and it made me laugh. Was the universe sending me a message I needed to hear again? Had Mom, who'd left us a few years back, made sure I'd eventually rediscover this treasure? And, wow, did my fixation on identity and class really start so young?

It seems the seeds of this book were planted all those years ago when my 20-year-old self was probably too defensive or embarrassed to hear my mother's message. Today, I get it. As a mother of five, like Mom, I understand how difficult it is to balance the impulse to protect our children with the necessity of letting them learn their own way.

We want them to be kind and caring stewards in the world while they figure out what they can and can't control and who they are apart from others. We want them to live a rich life and trust they'll figure out what that looks like no matter what's in their bank account.

Mom, thank you for your wisdom, caring, and words. May they be paid forward.

What is a Rich Life?

> *Happiness lies not in finding what is missing, but in finding what is present.* - Tara Brach

* * *

When I was little, I was obsessed with a "poor little rich boy" named Richie Rich, a popular comic book character who was the richest kid in the world. Everything about his life was tied to money, including his middle name, a dollar sign.

As a 10-year-old, I loved to snuggle in with a Richie Rich adventure after school as I ate my favorite treat of vanilla ice cream mixed with chocolate sauce. In addition to my personal sundae, I loved the outsized adventures of this goofy character in a bow tie and how he navigated relationships in his crazy world of opulence. On one hand, Richie had everything money could buy. On the other hand, this kind and charitable soul often felt lonely and neglected as he figured out how money related to love and connection. For example, whenever Richie would give his girlfriend, Gloria Glad, an expensive gift, she would refuse it and criticize the display of wealth despite his efforts to downplay it.

I wasn't alone in my Richie obsession. The series became the most popular for the Harvey Comics franchise in the 1970s and was later turned into a comic strip, TV show, and movie starring Macaulay Culkin. Perhaps the creators wanted us to ponder what it means to be rich or to live a rich life given our fascination with wealth. After all, we run races around the world, compete to survive on desert islands, play the lottery, and buy bitcoin, all in hopes of a financial windfall and the promise of a better life.

Unfortunately, the Hollywood version of a rich life is a mirage. It doesn't help us manage the day-to-day grind of paying bills, flipping burgers, or talking about money with a loved one. We aspire to be rich, yet we have different views on what being rich means. We think we're broken or that we're less than others if we don't have as much money. We connect our self-worth to our net worth.

* * *

There's no question that money is an important ingredient in meeting basic needs like housing, healthcare, food, and utilities. We need it to pay for transportation and to access services that improve our quality of life. It's nearly impossible to imagine a life in which money isn't a critical resource. Beyond that, where does it fit into the broader definition of a 'rich life'? Perhaps it's not quite as central as we often assume. As the Beatles famously sang, "I don't care too much for money, money can't buy me love." As one of my coaches once told me, "There are many forms of payment. Cash is just one of them."

This is where Positive Money comes in.

Positive Money makes it possible to live a rich life when you're tuned into what feels enriching. It separates the numbers from what you make them mean. It gives you a point of reference for how you want to be in your relationship with money and offers practices for sorting that out. If all goes well, you'll clarify what matters most and establish a reliable system to guide your daily money decisions.

* * *

Let's face it. Money doesn't care how hard you or I work. It doesn't know how smart or deserving you are or pay attention to whether you have enough to pay your bills or deal with an emergency. It has no opinion about being used for good or evil and happily complies with the policies, practices, and priorities we set for it. This means *we are as much the problem as we are the solution*. We have the choice to stick with the status quo or to embrace opportunities for change at a personal and societal level. As Winston Churchill once said, "No one ever finds life worth living – one has to make it worth living."

If you want your life to be one worth living, then consider Positive Money as a guidebook to a rich life by helping you:

- *Feel more confident and comfortable in money conversations.*
- *Be better prepared to navigate financial challenges.*
- *Be less judgmental of yourself and others.*
- *Focus on what counts now and for future generations.*
- *Accept what you can't control and be curious about what you can.*
- *Understand what triggers you around money.*
- *Move from fear to fearless in all things financial.*

How to Use This Book

> *My purpose: to lift your spirit and to motivate you.* - Mavis Staples

* * *

In the following pages, I share my story of finding grace in this messy place of money, and how Positive Money grew out of that experience. Then, in Part I, *About Positive Money*, I walk you through the three dimensions of Positive Money: the principles, process, and practice. I also explain why our relationship with money is so important and how you can tell that Positive Money is for you. In Part II, *The 7 Principles*, you learn about each principle through relatable scenarios, gain insight into patterns and tendencies, and see what it looks like before and after the application of the principle. In Part III, *Positive Money at Work*, you'll find simple practices and resources to foster a healthy and positive relationship with money.

If you're ready to jump in, I suggest you bookmark the Positive Money Club at www.positivemoneyclub.com. You can use your book order confirmation to access a variety of book bonuses.

As management expert, Ken Blanchard reminds us, "When you're interested in something, you do it only when it's convenient. When you're committed to something, you accept no excuses, only results."

Let's get committed.

Finding Grace in this Messy Place

> *The next message you need is always right where you are.*
> - Ram Dass

I was in my early fifties when I realized my relationship with money was messing with my dreams. It started one night when I couldn't sleep or shake a conversation I'd had earlier with my wife. We'd been talking about my frustration with my current stint as an executive director running a startup with a tight budget. Though I'd thought it would be fulfilling work, it was slow going for little pay. I wasn't happy. The effort felt herculean and risky and reminded me of the reasons why I had left the nonprofit sector earlier in my career.

One of my dreams was to become a successful entrepreneur. I'd been raised to think of creative ways to generate income and had run a freelance design business earlier in my career to be more present for raising kids. This had worked quite well until an unexpected divorce and midlife crisis changed the landscape of life financially and otherwise, so I went back to work full-time. Now, almost ten years into a new relationship and a set of twins added to the three children from my previous marriage, I was back to the question of whether to rekindle my dream and, if so, when.

Sleep wasn't something I usually struggled with. As a parent, I was used to grabbing some shut-eye whenever possible. This was different. My heart was racing. My mind was spinning. Did I really want to start and grow my own business? Should I accept my wife's offer to support me in the venture? Was I being delusional about my capacity or commitment to really make a go of it? What if I failed?

While these questions rolled across my mind like a ticker tape, I wondered how I could move forward and realize my dream if I was paralyzed by fear and self-doubt. That's when it hit me.

I was *expecting* to fail. Even worse, I was expecting someone to save me when I did.

* * *

Growing Up

I grew up in a tight-knit family of five girls and my parents in Jackson Hole, Wyoming. We lived on a bench overlooking Wilson, a small, unincorporated town of 200 settled at the base of Teton Pass. Our childhood was blessed with activities like horseback riding, overnight camping, and running in the forests and fields around our house. After attending local public schools through my first year of high school, I followed in the footsteps of my older sisters in attending a private school in Colorado until I graduated in 1976. After a gap year spent teaching cross-country skiing in New Hampshire, I went to college on the East Coast and eventually made my way to Washington, DC, in my early twenties. This was the same age my parents were when they got married in 1949 in the tiny Chapel of Transfiguration under the shadow of the Grand Tetons.

My parents had met on the East Coast, where they both attended elite liberal arts colleges and were working at a summer resort in Vermont. At the time, Dad was recovering from an aneurysm he'd suffered on his first day back from his mission as a bomber pilot in the South Pacific. After two years of intense therapy, he was able to walk though his right side remained partially paralyzed. He'd been athletic growing up, so this change in life was significant.

Nevertheless, Dad was intent on following through with his plan to head out to Wyoming in the fall to work on a dude ranch. His goal was to live in the Rocky Mountains after traveling there as a teen with his father. John, Sr. was a businessman, avid skier, and one of the founders of the National Ski Patrol. At one point he worked for the Union Pacific Railroad and was on the team designing the first ski chairlift in Sun Valley, Idaho. Even though Dad couldn't ski, the mountains, cold powder snow, and ranch life beckoned.

Mom was a beauty and clearly drawn to this handsome young man who looked like a combination of Jimmy Stewart and Gregory Peck and was as sweet as they come. She had grown up with a single mom living in New York City as a bookkeeper and voice coach. Though she enjoyed the countryside, she had her sights on a life in the big city, where she planned to return after the summer for a job as a copy editor at the New York Times.

Needless to say, they fell madly in love, and plans changed.

The story goes that after their summer romance, it was six months before Mom heard from Dad. Eventually, his eloquent letters started to arrive and included an invitation to join him the following summer. Whether it was the prospect of a short visit to the mountains or a long future with a man whose charm radiated like the northern lights, Mom accepted the invitation. When she landed in Rock Springs, Wyoming, dressed to the nines in her city best, no one thought she would stay, much less thrive in the rough-and-tumble community of scrappy idealists up north. Little did they know.

Our parents carved out a living for themselves and their daughters in the growing tourist hub despite the challenges of living in a small town. Dad, nicknamed "Juany" because he was born in Mexico City where his parents were stationed at the time, started out driving a horse-drawn taxi, worked at the lumber store, and later taught himself to design homes. Mom, "Georgie," stayed at home to raise us, making sure we were busy learning inside and outside the classroom.

Both volunteered and were central to community life, whether it was serving on a school board or planning commission, creating a local art association and science school, or timing at ski meets. It was a whole community of doers. Their friends founded the local newspaper, started a world-renowned clothing company, opened a now-famous outdoor leadership school, and gained distinction as grizzly bear researchers.

* * *

It's hard to imagine a richer life even though I know it wasn't always easy.

As kids, we had everything we needed, though we never felt overindulged or spoiled. If anything, Mom would remind us of the "starving children in Africa" if we didn't eat our food, and there were lots of hand-me-downs. She was the money minder who had been taught to be thrifty and resourceful by her mother as it was just the two of them growing up. She was an equal partner for Dad, who was self-employed and the breadwinner.

Early on, creativity and enterprise were valued, especially by Mom, who was an artist herself. She taught us how to paint, sew, knit, crochet, make elk horn buttons, weave belts, and fashion jewelry – all with the incentive to sell our work at the local craft fair, keep us busy during long winter nights, or both. To raise money, my sisters and I would wash cars, raise 4H cows, and babysit. At age 8, I had a lemonade stand called The Pink Moose, painted pink with a jigsaw cutout of a moose head with antlers nailed to the top. A "Get your juice at the Pink Moose" sign invited the few drivers along our small country road to stop for a 10-cent cup of pink joy. Later I worked as a maid, a waitress, and a sales clerk at the local sporting goods store – all before heading off to college, where I washed dishes to help with tuition.

When our parents and some friends wanted to protect a ranch in the heart of the valley from being sold to developers, they scraped enough funds together to make a downpayment. The following years were stressful financially. I was either too young or too down the line of sisters at the time to understand the pressures though I was aware they existed. It wasn't that Mom and Dad didn't share money challenges or deny us information. It was more that managing money was a challenging part of life and they didn't want to burden us.

Buying the ranch on top of owning a home and acreage in another part of the valley tagged us as rich even though we didn't think of ourselves that way. If anything, we were learning that being rich was bad. Dad would complain about the greed coming into the valley, and locals would bemoan the impact of the new wealth. There was a growing income gap in the county as Wyoming's favorable tax laws and the creation of a new ski resort attracted those with disposable income. Even as donors were funding projects my parents helped to create, there was tension around it – the new wealth came with mixed emotions and expectations. I remember feeling confused about where we stood in the lineup. If we were rich, wasn't that bad? Can one be rich and *good*?

***

Back to the sleepless night. I acknowledged my self-defeatist tendencies. I started thinking about my mother's letter again. Was all of this related? Had she identified my inner conflict all those years ago?

I considered my options once more.

On one hand, I was eager to take my wife up on her offer. I'd learned to accept help early on. As a 6-year-old, when I was stuck on a sewing or knitting project, I could turn to my sisters or Mom to help me get unstuck. When I went away to college and needed money, my parents would do what they could. Despite their concerns, they were there for me when I went through a divorce. I always appreciated the help, but part of me hated feeling helpless.

Which brings us to the other hand. I was desperate to prove that I could do something on my own and make a good income doing it. I aspired to build a business that could scale without a lot of staff and to apply practices that I'd learned as a student of organization development over the years. There was a problem with this aspiration, however. A reason my faith wavered. The dirty little secret: I was terrible at sales, and money made me anxious. Though I'd been a steady earner, I'd never been a big one. This, combined with a fear of failure, left me in a state bordering on panic.

The next morning, I sought relief at the library. I hoped to find answers in the business or finance sections, though I already had a good number of books on these topics at home. Unfortunately, it was looking like a failed expedition until my eyes landed on a small book that would change my life, *Making Peace with Money* by Jerrold Mundis. As I scanned the pages, I realized how much of the book was resonating. He wasn't just talking about the mechanics of money; he was talking about our relationship with money – how we assign meaning to this resource and make it a source of pain and suffering no matter how much or how little we have.

I'd never heard of money being described in this way. Mundis opened my eyes to a new dimension of financial life driven by emotions and beliefs.

My Rich Life Today

Finding grace in this messy place has taught me that a rich life is always available as long as we're available to it. I was a seeker and, in many ways, continue to be – often looking for the greener grass. After living and working for a year in Rome as an art director for a children's fashion magazine, I married a journalist and we went on to have three beautiful daughters while I ran a freelance graphic design business out of our house.

In my early forties, life took a few dramatic turns when I went back to school to earn a master's in education and human development, changed careers, fell in love with a woman, and got divorced. Needless to say, it was a difficult time as I struggled with this new identity and the fallout from the disruption.

Eventually, I learned how important self-love and self-worth is to living a rich life. In the process, my wife and I welcomed a set of twins and found our footing as a blended family with five kids, all the while holding down separate careers and businesses.

From that time until now, 20 years later, I've also learned how important our relationship with money is, especially as we navigate big life decisions and transitions. If you always rely on others to take care of you, what happens when you're finally on your own? If you're raising a family or growing a business and you avoid money conversations, what opportunities might you be squandering? If you think you still need more to live a rich life, what do you need?

These are the kinds of questions I explore through my money mindset and mental fitness coaching, writing, and product development. For example, I created Pizza Money® to teach youth and parents how to raise money-smart kids, and I plan to reissue many of those resources as I grow the Positive Money Club. I've also worked with women entrepreneurs to help them craft and implement business models and platforms that evolve around the impact they want to make in the world.

Yes, life is messy. Finding grace in this messy place isn't always easy, but it can be rewarding. It's taught me that fear is a powerful teacher and that love conquers all. It's taught me that we can do hard things and come out better for doing so. It's taught me that money is both simple and complicated, just like the humans who depend on it.

I couldn't be here today without the support of others. I'm grateful for my family of origin who taught me to be of service and that adversity breeds character. I'm grateful for my wife, who's stood beside me through thick and thin, and for our children, who are growing up to do amazing things in the world.

Further, I'm grateful for the many clients and colleagues I've worked with over the years who are leaders, entrepreneurs, and activists doing important work. This book contains some of their stories as well as references to like-minded movements like Conscious Capitalism which claims that businesses should operate ethically while they pursue profits.[1]

Positive Money is my way to find grace in a messy place. It's a choice, a practice, a philosophy, and a commitment. May it transform your life as much as it has mine.

---

1. Learn more at https://www.consciouscapitalism.org/

Part One

About Positive Money

"So often in life, things that you regard as an impediment turn out to be great, good fortune." - Ruth Bader Ginsburg

The mission of the Positive Money Club is to empower individuals and organizations to have a positive, productive, and purposeful relationship with money.

Unfortunately, money is stressful for many no matter what's in our bank accounts. A growing number of us don't have enough to meet basic needs like housing and food. Costs for health and child care continue to climb and economic disparity abounds. Emotionally, we feel ashamed of how much we make or don't make, anxious in money conversations, or worried about our financial security.

Given that money doesn't have a say in how it's used, the buck stops with you and me. We make decisions every day that drive how we show up for money and ultimately for ourselves and others. This can feel negative or positive depending on what you bring to the table and choose to focus on.

This is why I created the 7 Principles of Positive Money. I wanted a simple way to guide financial decisions that are intentional and values-based. I wanted them to be accessible and relatable so anyone could apply them whether buying groceries or creating a will.

In Part I, I share the premise and promise of Positive Money and common ways we relate to money. I then walk you through how Positive Money works, the role of mental fitness, and why we need Positive Money today.

Chapter 1

The Premise and Promise of Positive Money

> *Once you replace negative thoughts with positive ones, you'll start having positive results.* - Willie Nelson

Positive Money is a philosophy for living in relationship with money that feels positive and leads to favorable results. It's a shortcut for busy moms, stressed-out business owners, and anyone else who wants to live a rich life from the inside out. It's an offering to those who have yet to cross over to a place of acceptance, curiosity, and forgiveness.

You make financial decisions that align with who you are, what you want, and the impact you desire for yourself and others at home and at work.

Whenever I share this vision with others — even before I explain it further — I hear, "I need that." Often, it's followed by awkward laughter or a look of common understanding that money is a loaded topic despite it being a simple medium of exchange.

Money *is* a loaded topic. It's a source of identity, power, and shame. It can be a blessing and a curse in our relationships, communities, and societies. It's an opportunity and a restriction. Something we need and wish we didn't.

These truths are shared all across the economic spectrum and can leave us with mixed feelings about money. We want to be free of the grip that it has over our lives and to embrace all that it makes possible. We want to feel secure and able to live our values and have systems that support us even if we have few assets.

In essence, we want to live a rich life.

The Premise

Have you ever purchased a lottery ticket in hopes of winning millions of dollars? What did you fantasize about? *My life would be so much easier. I could just do what I wanted all day long. I could finally pay off debt and just not worry about money anymore.*

You're not alone in hoping for a windfall and imagining a life without money anxiety.

In the fall of 2022, the USA Powerball lottery had a jackpot worth over one billion dollars. While it's nearly impossible to resist spending $2 on a chance to win the jackpot, it's also nearly impossible to win. Yet we do it – sometimes for fun and sometimes because it's our only hope.

We assume a financial windfall will make life easier, but there's no guarantee it will make it richer. Why? Because the virtues of a rich life like joy, unconditional love, and connection are priceless. Our hearts melt when we witness vulnerability. Something special happens when we experience generosity. As Gloria Glad from the Richie Rich comics reminds us – love and friendship are not commodities.

This is the premise of Positive Money. You can live a rich life no matter what's in your bank account when you focus on what makes it rich and whether your relationship with money is in service of that intention. While we know money is an important factor, we often expect it to do more than it's capable of: make us happy, save our marriages, get us a job, etc. We can expect it to make life easier when it actually might make it more complicated.

The point here is that Positive Money is about how you relate to money, not about money itself. When you're in the Positive Money zone, you come from a place of generosity, grace, and gratitude instead of fear, shame, and blame. You have compassion for yourself and others in this messy place of money and the skills for responding to the mess. You want a healthy relationship with money that fosters greater ease and flow and produces positive outcomes. You want this for yourself and the greater good, knowing that our only control is over how we show up.

The Promise

The promise of Positive Money is that it can change how you think, act, and feel about money so you experience:

- *Greater ease and flow in your financial life.*
- *More confidence in responding to money challenges.*
- *Empowerment and ownership in your relationship with money.*
- *Self-acceptance.*
- *Connection to what matters most.*

With Positive Money your tomorrow could look quite different than your today.

- *Today, you avoid paying bills and wonder how you'll ever get out from under the mountain of debt you're carrying. Tomorrow, you're debt-free and paying bills on time.*
- *Today, you don't know what to say to your children when they ask to buy something outside the family budget.*

Tomorrow, you feel confident in talking to your kids about money.

- *Today, you feel frustrated with the spending habits of a family member or friend. Tomorrow, you feel comfortable having important money conversations with those you care about.*

In the following pages, you'll learn more about Positive Money and how it works. But before we get there, let's look at why our relationship with money matters and how you know Positive Money is for you.

Chapter 2

You and Money

> *There is a gigantic difference between earning a great deal of money and being rich.* - Marlene Dietrich

Your relationship with money is as important as money itself – or even more so. Why? Because what you think and feel about money – your money mindset – has an impact on your earning, spending, saving, and giving. It defines who you are, what you have access to, and even your self-worth. The more you understand your particular money mindset and what you can and can't control, the closer you'll get to experiencing your version of a rich life.

Our relationship with money involves characteristics that define our human-to-human relationships. These characteristics range from abusive to loving and show up in subtle or obvious ways. They can have little to do with how much or how little money we have. Rather, they're linked to early experiences with money, how we learned to cope in the world, and the set of values we've developed. Sadly, even the most wealthy are not immune to money problems. They often struggle with guilt, fear of failure, or faith that they're loved for reasons beyond their wealth.

I sort these relationships with money into four main categories. Yours may fit into more than one. Let's start with the most negative.

Adversarial

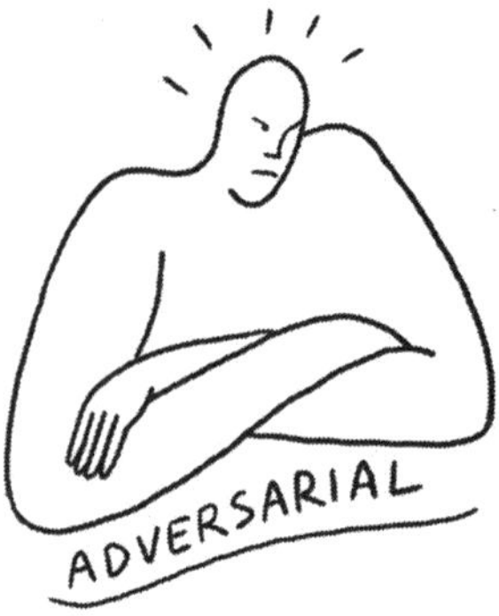

An adversarial relationship with money is one where you and money are at odds. You don't work well as a team. More often than not, you resent it for the control it has over how you feel about yourself and others. You don't like that it determines what you can or can't do, and you feel helpless in changing that paradigm. On one hand, you're aware of how important and necessary money is. On the other hand, you want to be free of the power it wields. You may even feel beat up by money.

If your relationship with money is adversarial or antagonistic, you may have tried to change it, but your strategies haven't worked. You tell yourself that you just need to be different, better, or work harder to be an equal player, but the bar seems to rise every time you try. You may get jealous of others with more money than you and feel worse about yourself or money as a result.

Ambivalent

An ambivalent relationship with money is one where you're not sure how to make sense of it. The relationship is marked by uncertainty, driven by an unsatisfied desire for something that feels right. You respect money and want to feel in charge of it but don't feel confident in how to manage it or clear on the role you want it to play in your life.

Part of you appreciates all that money does and can do in your life while another part resists the energy and attention it demands. You probably want more of it in your life, given how you feel about it. You envy or judge others who have a better relationship with money. Your conflicted feelings about money keep you from achieving your dreams.

If your relationship with money is ambivalent, you may have learned growing up that money is stressful or negative in some way. You might feel out of your depth in managing it, so you avoid dealing with it. Stepping outside the accepted norms around money in your family or culture causes stress.

Apathetic

An apathetic or indifferent relationship with money is one of ignoring or not caring about money. Instead of mixed feelings about money, your feelings are blah. It doesn't inspire you or interest you, and maybe it even annoys you. You wonder why it needs so much attention or doesn't show up on its own. You have other things you would rather focus on.

If you see yourself in this relationship with money, you probably avoid it because it makes you uncomfortable or you think others focus on it too much. If you were once in an adversarial or ambivalent relationship with money, this new apathetic relationship could be a result of not wanting to fall back into old patterns. It's just easier to not deal with it.

Abundant

An abundant or positive relationship with money is one driven by gratitude, generosity, and grace. You and money are good friends and have a healthy respect for one another. You take deliberate actions to take care of it. You're intentional about how you want to be in the relationship, so you don't take money for granted or have negative feelings toward it. If anything, you appreciate all it does for you and those around you and take actions that keep it flowing and growing, knowing that it needs to flow to be of benefit.

If you have an abundant relationship with money, you may have learned to manage it earlier in life, so you feel comfortable with the natural ebbs and flows. You know where you stand with it and have a healthy understanding of what it can and can't do in terms of making you happy. You know how to avoid it being stressful, and when you do feel stressed, you're equipped to manage it.

* * *

The goal of Positive Money is to have an abundant relationship with money. My mission is to help you achieve that goal. Unfortunately, many of us would place our relationship with money somewhere in the first three categories, describing it as adversarial, ambivalent, apathetic, or some combination of the three. We might have moments when it feels abundant, but those moments are fleeting.

When I started on this journey, I had an ambivalent relationship with money. Sometimes it bordered on adversarial. I would let money define who I was or my value in the world. I was a "good" person if I worked in the nonprofit space and a "bad" person if I worked for a for-profit company. I wanted to prove I could make more money, yet I was also afraid of the responsibility, especially of failure. Those fears prevailed until I realized I needed to face them.

As you know, relationships can change on a dime. When and if you decide to face your fears, or whatever stops you from having an abundant relationship with money, you'll not only change but transform your financial life. You'll learn to step back and get curious without judgment, assess what's true or false, and move forward with intention. You'll learn to separate what you can control from what you can't. Ultimately, you'll find grace in this messy place and be the better for it.

Chapter 3

How Positive Money Works

> *If you change the way you look at things, the things you look at change.* - Wayne Dyer

The 3 P's of Positive Money

Positive Money begins with the end in mind — a positive relationship with money that fosters a rich life. What that rich life looks and feels like is up to you and may change along the way. Wherever you start or end up, the principles, process, and practice of Positive Money will serve you along the way.

- The **principles** become your guiding philosophy.
- The **process** is about pausing when you encounter a challenge so you can choose your next Positive Money move based on a principle that resonates.
- The **practice** puts and keeps you in the Positive Money zone so you have what you need to respond in a way that feels positive.

The Principles

The 7 Principles of Positive Money draw from what I've learned in my 60+ years on this planet, where money is a critical resource and one that is prized and rewarded. I wish I had these principles earlier in my life when money was a source of stress or limitation, and I didn't know why. I would have felt more confident in having difficult financial conversations or managing money had I had a framework or set of principles like the ones listed below.

Each principle can stand on its own or work in tandem with others to help you make wise money decisions in real time. For example, a dear friend invites you out to dinner. You know they earn less than you do, so you make a mental note that you'll pay the check. You might assume this is a Positive Money move. But is it? How often do you end up paying even if someone else invites you out or offers to pay? If so, what assumptions are you making? What would it look or feel like if you let them pay this time?

I offer this example because assuming you'll pay for others, even when they invite you out, can rob them of the joy of giving or enabling. Also, as generous as you are or like to be, there may be part of you that finds it difficult to receive. In this case, you could clarify expectations. If your friend insists on paying for both of you, say thank you without qualification and notice how you feel. It can take a while to build the muscle of receiving, especially if you don't use it much.

The following is a list of the principles. You'll learn how to use them in the next section under process. In Part II, you'll learn more about each principle and what it looks like when they're applied.

Positive Money is…

1. **A choice.** *When you choose Positive Money, you choose a relationship with money driven by love rather than fear.*
2. **Generational.** *When you're aware of the beliefs and behaviors you inherit and pass along, you're more intentional about your actions today.*
3. **Serves a higher good.** *When you're grounded by a higher good, you have the interests and needs of others in mind.*
4. **Aligns head, heart, and habit.** *When your thoughts, feelings, and actions related to money are aligned, you experience ease and flow.*
5. **An act of giving and receiving.** *When you give and receive equally, you experience the power of connection.*
6. **Causes no harm.** *When you understand how your money choices cause harm to yourself and others, you take action to mitigate that harm.*
7. **A practice.** *When you practice Positive Money, you apply the principles to daily financial decisions with mindfulness and compassion.*

The Process

The process of Positive Money is to pause, notice, and choose your next step using positive or generative questions to guide your way. When faced with a financial conundrum or challenge like the one above, you pause for at least six seconds to give your rational brain a chance to process your feelings and access your thoughts. You can then scan the list of principles and choose one that resonates, or simply ask a question like, "What matters most right now?"[1]

The concept behind this process is to give yourself time to adjust your actions after considering what you really want or need at the time. Viktor Frankl, a Jewish-Austrian psychiatrist, called this the space between stimulus and response. "In that space is our power to choose our response. In our response lies our growth and our freedom."[2]

Let's imagine that you have an upcoming conversation about your salary with your supervisor. You're nervous about it, and you don't want your nerves to hold you back from asking for the raise you determined would put you on the same level as your peers.

In preparing for the meeting, you take time to pause and notice how you're feeling. While in this space, you ask yourself what matters most about the conversation. This question might be enough to help you feel calmer and gain more clarity on your approach. If not, you could scan the list of principles and choose one that resonates. The third principle about serving a higher good could be a great reminder about why you're in this line of work and position in the first place.

The following are a few more examples from my clients.

- *One likes to pause and check in with how a money decision aligns with her head, heart, and habit which is the fourth principle of Positive Money. If something feels out of sorts, she looks for opportunities for alignment. The more of this she does, the more she trusts her internal compass.*
- *Another favors principle six about causing no harm. She says it's a shortcut to knowing whether a money action or decision is right for her. If she feels pressured or ill-prepared, she*

knows to advocate for her needs by taking her time or checking in with her self-judgment.

Positive Questions

Positive or generative questions are thought-provoking and at the heart of the Positive Money process. These questions come from a place of genuine curiosity and help us navigate our day even if we aren't conscious of them. *What time is it? What should I wear? Where are my keys?* In *The Art of the Question*, author Marilee Adams reminds us that this is our natural state of being. "Since we basically walk the paths in life prescribed by our questions, it makes sense to ask those which can take us where we want to go."[3]

While this state of inquiry comes naturally, it can get shut off or turned down when expressed aloud. Think back on the toddler whose litany of "Why" questions is eventually shushed by an impatient parent. In school, I remember the teachers getting annoyed by too many questions or my fear of looking dumb in front of my peers. We're also not taught how to ask questions outside of research or scientific settings even though they're at the heart of discovery and innovation. In our educational and workplace settings, we're more rewarded for coming up with solutions than for raising questions. We think asking questions will make us seem inadequate or high maintenance or will delay a project when, more often than not, our rush to find a solution can cost us in the end.

This is why Positive Money uses questions designed to uncover existing strengths, advantages, and opportunities that might otherwise get missed. The questions are inspired by Appreciative Inquiry (AI), a practice that taps into collective wisdom and turns on the creative or problem-solving parts of our brains when we need solutions to complex problems.[4] For example, one of the five core principles of AI is the Positive Principle which claims that positive questions lead to positive change.

Positive or generative questions often start with How, What, or Where instead of Why which can lead someone down a road of self-critique. Once you pause and notice that you aren't entirely sure how to respond, you can ask questions like:

- *How might this be a Positive Money move?*
- *What matters most about this situation?*
- *What does love look like here?*

These questions and others like them can help unlock your greatest strengths and true self in any situation. When it comes to money, they help you connect to your core values and what you truly want or need at the moment. For example, if you really want a new car, take a moment to notice the thoughts and feelings you have about it. What about your thoughts and feelings seem positive and what seems negative? If your future self argues against it because it will put you into debt, what might your present self say? How might you resolve the differences?

Getting an idea out of your head can be challenging, especially one related to a desire. However, when you commit to this process – when you choose Positive Money – you tune into what serves you and turn off what doesn't.

> *Knowing oneself comes from attending with compassionate curiosity to what is happening within.* - Gabor Maté

The Practice

The practice of Positive Money is about exploring your relationship with money in three separate categories: Head, Heart, and Habit. Each of these dimensions of your being drives your doing.

When they're aligned, which is the fourth principle of Positive Money, you experience greater ease and flow not just in your relationship with money but in others areas of life as well. The practice helps you better understand these dimensions so you can jump in and course correct when you experience moments of misalignment.

How you intervene directs you back to the principles of Positive Money, engages the process of pausing, noticing, and choosing your next action, and leverages your mental fitness. Suggestions for building your mental fitness are included in Chapter 7 under Positive Money Practices.

* * *

Head

Your money mindset is the set of beliefs and attitudes you have about earning, spending, saving, and giving. The better you get at identifying these beliefs and attitudes and where they show up, the more capable you will be in developing and maintaining a Positive Money mindset.

One way to learn about your mindset is to listen to the stories you tell yourself about what's going on. Is it fact or is it fiction? For example, the fact may be that you have $100 in your checking account. The story you tell yourself is that you're bad at managing your money or that your employer needs to pay you more. You look for evidence to prove you're right. You're skeptical of anyone telling you otherwise, or you flat-out disagree. It becomes a vicious cycle of rinse and repeat, leaving little room for new perspectives or experiences.

Money stories form over time. We hear direct messages like "Money doesn't grow on trees" or more subtle messages that nonetheless shape our identity and class. As women, we're told it's unladylike to talk about money or that there

are only certain jobs for us. As men, we're told to be breadwinners and expected to be good with money. Though those narratives change with the generations, they endure when they're passed down. For example, it's not uncommon for women to be under-earners because they think asking for more money is selfish or finances are someone else's responsibility. Men who seek a different path can feel less 'manly' if they don't live up to certain financial expectations.

Once you identify your money stories, you start to notice those of others. Again, they can be hidden in full view and wrapped up in a larger narrative about merit, worthiness, and relationships. For instance, a friend once told me that he was a picky eater when he was little. His dad would punish him when he refused to eat what was served for family dinner. He would "get the belt" and was denied any snacks the next day. Imagine the trauma associated with a basic need like food and how it could translate into resistance to anyone, especially an authority figure, telling him what to do.

Our mindset can be open or closed. In *Mindset: The New Psychology of Success,* Carol Dweck calls this a growth versus fixed mindset. She asserts that a growth mindset is essential to fulfilling our potential as parents, business owners, students, and partners. "The passion for stretching yourself and sticking to it, even (or especially) when it's not going well, is the hallmark of the growth mindset. This is the mindset that allows people to thrive during some of the most challenging times in their lives." The fixed mindset stops us from moving forward and discourages growth.[5]

With our money mindset, the lines are not always clear. We can have a growth mindset but get caught in patterns that seem fixed. For example, if you believe you're not good enough, undeserving, or always need to be the provider, you can feel at war with yourself. On one hand, we know it's possible to change and may want to change, but those snarly beliefs hold us back. I once came up with the hashtag #sicko'myself after a period of swearing I'd get on top of my finances only to end up falling short or regressing because of negative beliefs I hadn't shed.

* * *

Heart

Our emotions and feelings serve as powerful signaling mechanisms. We may *think* we're making a Positive Money move only to discover that our body is sending a different message. The more we learn about these mechanisms and how to build our emotional intelligence, the better equipped we are to communicate our needs around money and to regulate and cope.

One of my favorite resources is an organization called Six Seconds, which provides an interactive model you can use to learn about emotions as well as an assessment. The name of the emotional intelligence network comes from the power of the 6-second pause you can take when you're triggered by stress, so you can make a conscious decision about what to do or say next.[6]

Given that our focus is on money, the *heart* part of this practice is to remember that your reactions to money *are* emotional. The more you learn the language and vocabulary of emotions and the experiences that lead to them, the more adept you'll be at interpreting what you're feeling and identifying emotions in others.[7]

If you have an emotional response to a financial situation like asking for a raise or talking with your spouse about money, I suggest putting a hand on your heart, taking a few deep breaths, and trying to label the emotion or feeling. Once you're able to identify it, you have options for responding. For example, you can practice acceptance by acknowledging the facts and letting go of what you can't control. This is part of building your mental fitness, which I talk about in the next chapter.

* * *

Habit

Money habits are behaviors that repeat themselves whether you like them or not. These patterns show up in our relationship with money as both thoughts and actions. They can be so familiar that it never crosses our mind that they can be changed. Alternatively, we may have tried to change them and failed, and we're not sure why. If they're extreme or addictive, like gambling or hoarding money, they may signal more serious mental health issues that require a greater level of intervention.

A few examples of money habits include:

- *Saying yes every time a check-out clerk offers you 10 or 20 percent off your purchases if you open a store credit card.*
- *Buying yourself a treat after a difficult encounter or every morning after dropping the kids at school.*
- *Making purchases knowing that you'll return them.*

As G.K. Cheston famously said, "Don't ever take a fence down until you know the reason why it was put up." This is a good reminder that our habits serve us until they don't.

The following are ways to understand why we develop habits in the first place and what to focus on if we want to change them.

Money Saboteurs - When we're born, we're hard-wired with certain behaviors. Other behaviors we learn. Both matter. If you were a sensitive child growing up in an abusive household you learned to be hypervigilant. If you were ignored by your parents, you probably learned to earn love by excelling in school or doing all the right things. If you experienced fights over money growing up, it's likely you'll avoid money matters as an adult.

While these behaviors may have served us early on as survival mechanisms, over time they can become a source of stress, anxiety, self-doubt, and frustration. In the system of Positive Intelligence® created by Shirzad Chamine, these survival mechanisms are called "Saboteurs," and we all have them to one extent or another. The "Master Saboteur" or Judge is considered universal because you can count on it to remind you of your shortcomings, mistakes, and excuses. This Judge activates other "Accomplice Saboteurs" that can hijack your mind and get in the way of progress. The nine accomplices include the Hyper Achiever, Hyper Rational, Stickler, Pleaser, Victim, Controller, Restless, Hyper Vigilant, and Avoider.[8]

Though there are other assessments and ways to understand our money behaviors, I use the Positive Intelligence model because it offers a system for detecting the lies we tell ourselves and the tools for debunking those lies by building our mental fitness. On my website, I talk more about the role of mental fitness and offer resources on how to identify and quiet your money saboteurs.

Our Saboteurs can do a number on our financial life without us even knowing it. For example, when I first heard my Judge, she was menacing and mean. She was standing over me saying, "Who are you to make more money?" When my Hyper-Achiever Saboteur steps up, I hear, "No matter how hard you work, it won't be enough."

* * *

Once you're ready to let go of old patterns and adopt new ones, knowing how to do so effectively is helpful. One strategy is to focus on identity. The other is to leverage your mental fitness. Both have been critical to shifting outcomes in my life and the lives of my clients.

Identity - James Clear tells us in his book *Atomic Habits* that we often fail to change our habits because we try to change the wrong thing in the wrong way. If you only focus on an outcome like losing weight, you'll likely fail. If you start with your identity — your worldview, self-image, etc. — you're more likely to succeed. "Behavior that is incongruent with the self will not last. You may want more money, but if your identity is someone who consumes rather than creates, then you'll continue to be pulled toward spending rather than earning." In other words, you should focus on becoming a runner rather than on running a marathon.[9]

After you consider a new or updated identity, take small and simple steps to adopt the habits that support it. According to BJ Fogg, author of *Tiny Habits: The Small Changes that Change Everything,* this can be easier and more fun than you think.[10] He developed a methodology for changing behavior that works based on over 20 years of research and coaching 60,000 people. "There are three ways to change behavior: have an epiphany, change the environment, change habits in tiny ways."

Both Fogg and Clear advise habit stacking, adding a new habit next to the one you already enjoy. If you want to become a saver, what small changes can you make around your habit of buying a fancy coffee every day on the way to work? If you want to save more for retirement, can you set up a separate savings account at your bank so that every time you deposit a check, a certain percentage is automatically allocated to that account?

* * *

Whatever our strategy, Dr. Margaret E. Smith, the author of *Money: From Fear to Love*, argues that understanding what's at play in your relationship with money can move you from scarcity, lack, and fear to wealth, prosperity, and love. "How far we go depends on how much we allow money to teach us," she says. The more we understand our motivations and where we get tripped up, the more effective we will be in learning what we need to get the results we want.[11]

Adair

Adair is the mother of 8-year-old twins. She is also an entrepreneur and a leader in a professional community where members learn to unlock potential in groups through the art of facilitation. Adair volunteered to tell her story because of the transformation she's experienced since working on her relationship with money. When asked to describe that relationship today, Adair said it was multidimensional, important, and generative because it continues to teach her so much. "It's like any other relationship – it ebbs and flows."

It wasn't always like that.

For most of Adair's life, she had fears about money and even shame. "My parents would say to me I would need to marry a rich man because I appreciated nice things. I was on the overspending side, for sure." Even though she admits that she's always earned well and met her needs, she heard "chitter-chatter about money" in her head that was all about what she was doing wrong.

A few life events turned things around. One was when she and her husband tried to have a baby and discovered there were fertility issues. Facing significant expenses, she decided she wanted to "figure out how we could cash flow this" and started "getting really nitty-gritty and aggressively paying off debts." She paid more attention as if it was just another relationship in her life. "I was paying attention and using the system, but I also think a lot of it had to do with my mindset." She realized that if she paid more attention and focused on nurturing the relationship, there would be room for more prosperity.

The other realization she had was that she and her husband had different relationships with money. He refused to do the "Dave Ramsey thing" and sit down to do a budget. It was a source of frustration knowing how little control she had over his behavior or priorities. Though they were blessed with two beautiful girls, she and her husband would eventually divorce. Afterward, "a lot of that stuff lifted."

Being on her own helped Adair remain committed to reading and learning about money mindset. A game changer was when she considered her energy around money. "When I'm talking about money, paying a bill, or looking at my budget, I'm noticing how my energy is contracting versus expanding." She began to practice "a lot of gratitude" and curiosity, asking what spending money is making possible for her.

Her favorite question has been, "What would it take?" [12] *Instead of saying, "Oh shit, I'm in trouble.' I would ask myself what it would take to get $10,000 more a month for example." More importantly, instead of Adair trying to answer the question herself, she would put it out to the universe, tapping into a larger pool of energy. In addition, she's been deliberate about taking care of her money, telling it, "Hey, I really need you to go over there and stay put so I can pay my taxes."*

In addition to mindset work, Adair expressed the value of hanging out with others with shared values and aspirations. "I was raised to believe you had a job and a finite amount of time. Now I know so much more is possible, especially when you're ready and open to receiving it."

* * *

When I asked Adair for her thoughts on Positive Money, she said that she can see how others might think it's about dismissing negative emotions, responding to distress with false reassurances, or assuming you need to feel joy all the time. Not so. "If you're in a constant state of joy, or you're looking for that dopamine hit, that can be equally damaging."

Adair's story could be one of many in which identity is tied to beliefs and behaviors that have spanned generations. This is why the second principle is about being generational and is focused on what we inherit and pass down. When you're tuned into messages from the past and how they're driving actions in the present, you can shift the narrative and therefore the impact. At the very least, it makes for interesting conversations and opportunities for grace.

---

1. Learn more at https://www.6seconds.org/
2. Frankl, Viktor. *Man's Search for Meaning: An Introduction to Logotherapy.* Boston, Beacon Press, 1992.
3. Adams, Ph.D., Marilee. *The Art of the Question: A Guide to Short-term QUestion-Centered Therapy.* John Wiley & Sons, 1998.
4. Appreciative Inquiry was developed in the early 1990s by David Cooperrider and Suresh Srivastva at Case Western Reserve University.
5. Dweck, Ph.D., Carol S. *Mindset: The New Psychology of Success.* New York: Ballantine Books, 2008.
6. Learn more at https://www.6seconds.org/
7. Brown, Ph.D., LSW, Brené. *Atlas of the Heart: Mapping Meaningful Connection and the Language of Human Experience.* First Edition. New York: Random House, 2021.
8. Chamine, Shirzad. *Positive Intelligence.* Austin, Texas: Greenleaf Book Group, 2012.
9. Clear, James. *Atomic Habits: An Easy & Proven Way to Build Good Habits & Break Bad Ones.* New York: Penguin Random House, 2018.
10. Fogg, Ph.D., B.J. *Tiny Habits: Small Changes That Change Everything.* Houghton Mifflin Harcourt, 2020.
11. Smith, Margaret H. Smith, Ph.D. *Money: From Fear to Love.* Ennea Coaching, 2011.
12. The power of this question is noted in the book, "Influence Is Your Superpower" by Zoe Chance, who points out that most of us miss opportunities because we fail to ask it. https://www.npr.org/2022/02/02/1077522578/yale-professor-teaches-influence-and-she-says-its-your-superpower

Chapter 4

The Role of Mental Fitness

> *Your mind is your best friend. But it can also be your worst enemy.* – Shirzad Chamine

Mental fitness is our ability to think clearly and to make decisions effectively and efficiently. It's reaching and maintaining a state of well-being and cultivating our awareness of how we think, behave, and feel. It's an intentional practice of building our emotional and social intelligence, so we're better prepared to deal with challenges such as a teenager scraping the car door in a parking garage and running up an $800 repair bill that wasn't in our budget. As physical fitness supports our physical health, mental fitness supports our mental health. As we keep track of our physical fitness by counting our steps or monitoring our heart rate, we can measure our mental fitness by how balanced we feel mentally, or how quickly we recover from an emotional reaction.

As we learn more about the brain, we're finding that activities like meditation, reading, refocusing throughout the day, breathwork, rubbing our fingertips together, playing music, and walking can help boost our mental fitness because they strengthen those parts of our brain that serve us and quiet those parts that don't. Such activities teach us what monks have known for centuries: a calmer mind helps us navigate stress, work better with others, and tap into creativity and innovation. When we commit to a mental fitness practice, we build our mental strength and agility, as physical fitness builds muscle. The higher our fitness level, the more resilient we become.

* * *

I offer specific ways to build your mental fitness in Chapter 7 under Positive Money practices.

* * *

I first learned about the mind-body connection through my mother. When she was young, she was introduced to the philosophies of Rudolf Steiner, who was a guru for her mother. Steiner believed that the human being is a threefold being of spirit, soul, and body. He founded a spiritual movement called Anthroposophy that assumes that a child's creative, spiritual, and moral dimensions need as much attention as their intellectual ones.

Steiner's teachings would form the foundation for Waldorf education and draw my grandmother and 10-year-old mother to Basel, Switzerland, where Steiner taught. When the war broke out several years later, they had to return to the United States. Their appreciation for the teachings continued and likely inspired Mom's major in college, which was a study of the relationship between art and science.

I'm guessing that this spiritual instruction was also what spurred Mom and some of her friends during the New Age movement in the 70s to form a group we called the "woo-woos" because they liked to talk about spirituality and explore mystical practices. For some reason, this made me uncomfortable – likely because it was my job as a teenager to be embarrassed by my mother, or perhaps I just wasn't ready for such matters.

Despite my resistance, she invited me to listen to Deepak Chopra, who had come to town to talk about his theories on quantum healing. Though I had never heard of him or had no idea what he would talk about, I was taken in by the mix of ideas that drew from quantum mechanics, neuroscience, psychology, and philosophy. This was well before he appeared on *Oprah* in 1993 to discuss his book *Ageless Body, Timeless Mind,* and before he became one of the best-known and wealthiest figures in alternative medicine.

Growing Popularity of Mental Fitness

While Steiner, Chopra, Oprah, and others have emphasized the connections between mind and body for years, I only first learned the term "mental fitness" several years ago through Positive Intelligence® and later from celebrities like Prince Harry, the Duke of Sussex.

For example, in 2021, the Duke helped to popularize the concept when he assumed the role of Chief Impact Officer at BetterUp, a company that helps people lead more meaningful lives. In announcing his new role, he said, "I firmly believe that focusing on and prioritizing our mental fitness unlocks potential and opportunity that we never knew we had inside of us. As the Royal Marine Commandos say, 'It's a state of mind.' We all have it in us."

Measuring Mental Fitness

With the growing interest in mental fitness has come the desire to measure it. You can now buy devices that give you biofeedback when you meditate or track and record your sleep patterns. Positive Intelligence® has created an app and system that measure the relative strength of our "Sage" versus our "Saboteurs" that it calls our "PQ" or Positive Intelligence Quotient. When you do mental fitness exercises in the PQ gym, you build your PQ strength and up your score.

Mental Fitness and Money

The more I've worked on my relationship with money and with clients on theirs, the more I appreciate the power of mental fitness to help us change what we can, accept what we can't, and become more resilient in the process.

Sometimes this can take a while, and that's ok. Our bodies and minds can signal when we need help, not just in our financial lives but in our lives in general. Burnout is a serious problem faced by many who suffer from taking care of others, believing they're not enough, or having health problems that scream the need for self-care. Often these symptoms are signs of the need to heal in one way or the other. When we don't have a healthy relationship with ourselves, we can't have a healthy relationship with money.

As Raj Sisodia shares in his story below, a process of awakening is often where this healing starts.

Raj Sisodia

Raj is a founding member of Conscious Capitalism, a philosophy and a movement based on the premise that businesses should serve all significant stakeholders, including the environment. He is also a professor who has written over 100 academic articles and an author who has co-written several books that detail how companies can make the world better by the way they do business, which not only serves the planet and the human condition but also the bottom line.[1]

Ironically, while Raj was writing and teaching about how such organizations are needed today, he was burning himself out. Just before he was to publish The Healing Organization, *his mentors approached him and asked if he had done his own healing. Giving that important question the consideration it deserved, he pushed the book publication date back and began a journey of conscious awakening (as he calls it), taking time to revisit his past and to face traumas known and unknown, whether in his own experience or in the culture and times he grew up in. In describing the journey, he quotes Carl Jung, "Until you make the unconscious conscious, it will direct your life and you will call it fate."*

* * *

In telling his story, which will appear in his next book *Awaken: A Journey to Purpose, Wholeness & Healing*, Sisodia exemplifies the journey necessary to heal those parts of ourselves that tell us we're undeserving, inadequate, imposters, or in need of proving ourselves in some way to love or be loved. By extension, he argues that organizations can also reflect on their past and examine how they can help to heal instead of continuing practices that cause suffering.

For example, Jeff Bezos makes millions by prioritizing profit over people. Can you imagine if Amazon prioritized work conditions and employee engagement? What would it look like if Purdue Pharma, the maker of the highly addictive painkiller OxyContin, were more invested in ensuring proper use of their highly addictive drugs than making huge profits?

Raj and his partners in the Conscious Capitalism movement help us see that success indicators can be defined beyond mere profitability. This is where Conscious Capitalism overlaps with Positive Money. Both philosophies support the view that it's possible to live a rich life when the focus is on more than what's in a bank account.

When we choose Positive Money, we believe in spreading the wealth, taking care of the valuable resources we rely on, and prioritizing long-term sustainability over short-term gain. Though these concepts may seem more aspirational than realistic, Raj and others demonstrate that they're not just possible but necessary.

---

1. Learn more at http://rajsisodia.com/

Chapter 5

Why We Need Positive Money

> *You only live once, but if you do it right, once is enough.*
> - Mae West

On a recent summer evening, my wife and I jumped on our Vespa 350 and rode across the city to watch a preview of the documentary *Tipping the Pain Scale* and to listen to panelists talk about creative solutions to the significant and growing addiction crisis. One of the speakers was Marty Walsh, the current Secretary of Labor and former mayor of Boston, who openly declared during his campaign that he was an alcoholic and in recovery for over twenty years. His public declaration was considered risky, but he didn't care. He wanted to do all he could to fight the stigma of addiction and the crisis of substance use disorders affecting millions, not just on the streets but in our homes, schools, and workplaces.

We were there because our family has directly experienced the impact of these disorders. While riding through our teenager's old stomping grounds, we thought about the psychological and financial costs of this experience. At one point during those dark times, we took out a second mortgage on our house to pay off over $100,000 in fees for treatments that offered no guarantee of success. I became a certified recovery coach so I could learn more and help others, and we continue to support the movement, which needs each of us to step up where we can.

Our story is not unique. Dealing with unexpected emotional and financial blows like addiction, losing a job or home, dealing with a health or pet emergency, or going through a divorce is more the rule than the exception. In all cases, it helps to have safety nets like insurance and savings in place if at all possible. It's a practice of Positive Money in that you're taking care of your future self so your present self can focus on what really counts.

The Need

The need for Positive Money is personal and institutional. We're shouldering the blame and shame of our 'failures,' but all this takes place within systems that are failing us. Wages aren't keeping up with the cost of living, and income inequality has grown substantially over the last 30 years in the United States.[1] Even if we want to save, it's getting harder. A little more than a quarter of American households have a net worth of $5000 or less![2]

Though it's no fun to write or think about what this looks or feels like, I share a few examples because they underscore the alarming need for change.

- **Rising consumer debt and inability to save.** In 2020, the average American carried $92,727 in consumer debt. This included credit card balances, auto, and home loans, and personal or student loans.[3] During the first quarter of 2022, household debt rose by almost two percent.[4] In a recent survey by Bankrate, just 44% of Americans could cover an unplanned $1,000 expense from savings. More than one-third would need to borrow the money in some fashion, and nearly half say inflation is cutting into their savings for unplanned expenses.[5]

- **Costs of measuring up.** Whether it's a college education, a house, property, a car, or a pair of shoes, the pressures to measure up are real and fueled by peers, the media, and cultural norms. For example, we learn that a college degree is necessary and that one from an elite institution is best. The financial services industry is happy to support this belief by offering loans and credit cards to help make it happen, even if it can lead to years of financial hardship. By the end of 2021, the Federal Reserve estimated that Americans owed over $1.7 trillion in student loans.[6] The irony is that the earning power of recent graduates is low, which makes managing debt along with other costs prohibitive and can drive the graduate away from a career they love to one that pays more or offers better benefits.

- **Lack of financial literacy.** A consistent finding by the TIAA Institute-GFLEC Personal Finance Index (P-Fin Index) now in its sixth year of assessing financial literacy among the U.S. adult population confirms that many Americans function with a poor level of financial literacy. "On average, U.S. adults correctly answered only 50% of the index questions in 2022. Eighteen percent correctly answered over 75% of the index questions, while 23% correctly answered 25% or fewer of the questions."[7]

- **The unbanked and underbanked.** Nearly 16 million U.S. households qualify as "unbanked," meaning they don't have an account with a bank or financial institution. An additional 16% are "underbanked," meaning that they have a traditional bank account but use alternative financial services like paycheck lending and check cashing services that often impose higher fees and penalties.[8]If you lose cash, you're cash out of luck.

- **Complex personal finance industry.** In *Pound Foolish,* Helaine Olson writes about the dark side of personal finance. As a journalist and former financial columnist, she looked behind the curtain of the industry and called out the get-rich-quick schemes and the culture of commissions that make it hard to decide who benefits most. She tells the story of a friend who went to a financial advisor who, she assumed, was a fee-only planner. Instead, the friend received an 80-page report with recommendations that leaned heavily on commission-laden strategies that she and her husband couldn't afford.[9]

* * *

Living under these financial conditions and feeling ill-equipped can take a toll mentally and financially. In some cases, the impact is heartbreaking. For example, a good friend and fellow money coach Tammy Lally lost her brother to suicide. He'd been struggling financially for some time, had a history of addiction, and left behind a wife and daughter. After the devastation of the loss, my friend was determined to go back and learn more about her brother's struggles and how her efforts to help were ineffective or even counterproductive. She went on to do a Ted Talk about the experience and the epidemic of money shame as well as write a book called *Money Detox.*[10] Though this work won't bring her brother back, she hopes it will help others avoid the pitfalls of money shame and all that it entails mentally, physically, and financially.

When I watched Tammy's talk, I cried along with her. I felt for my friend and for the suffering that was present as much before her brother's death as it was afterward. It made me angry that meeting basic needs such as housing is increasingly difficult, especially for those with fixed or unsteady incomes. It's far too easy to blame the victim when what's needed is empathy, compassion, and practical solutions.

* * *

While Positive Money is needed on a personal level, it's also needed in business where profits are often prioritized over people and the environment. Before Covid-19 upended our lives, we knew that the income gap between the rich and everyone else was growing and that certain practices line the pockets of a few at the expense of many. For example, in 2020 in the United States, CEO pay jumped 15% among the one hundred largest companies while their global median pay flatlined. More than half of these companies rigged their own rules to inflate CEO pay — protecting the huge bonuses of top executives while their workers suffered.[11]

The pandemic tightened the screws. In early 2021, workers began to resign or not show up for work due to unsafe conditions or inadequate wages. In 2022, companies were scrambling to find workers who could afford to work or live at the wages offered. For example, in my hometown, the median price for a house topped $2 million. Teachers and other critical personnel among others are driving two hours to get to work. On top of that, property taxes went up an average of 30% in 2021. Even if you own a home or business as our family has since 1949, it's becoming prohibitive for many to live there.[12]

Meeting the Need

Given the long list of financial challenges, it's hard to imagine how Positive Money can make a dent – but it can. When you choose Positive Money, you focus on what you *can* control including the language you use, the assumptions you make, and how you show up.

For example, my wife and I took a trip to visit our youngest at college with the mission to close on a condo we had purchased for her. We had determined that it made more sense to buy instead of rent given how many years she expected to live in this city. At one point, my wife remarked teasingly about how spoiled our kids were. At first, I laughed and agreed. Then I thought about how negative that term was and how we were the ones doing the spoiling. I gently suggested that we use a different way to think about our gifting or investment, much like my mom decided not to call us 'little turds.'

Had I not done Positive Money work, I would have never noticed the words we were using, much less suggest more positive ones. It made me appreciate how helpful the principles can be at the moment. I was able to scan the list in my head and the one that popped up was the first one about choice. We had chosen to purchase the condo with good intentions and had done what we thought best by letting our daughter learn from the experience even if it was stressful at times. When I took a few minutes to remind myself of this, it not only readjusted my thinking but also my feelings. It also made me appreciate the benefits of learning how to have money conversations so more can benefit.

The following are different ways to do that in ways that can not only help you but can influence others.

Personal decisions - Each of your financial decisions have an impact, not just in your immediate life but on others downstream. When you keep money flowing, you ensure that others can put food on the table and keep the lights on. When you're more thoughtful of where or how you spend or accept money, you exercise a level of influence. When you make Positive Money moves, you make a positive influence on those around you.

Professional decisions - If you're a business owner, you have a range of choices around how you set up your company, make a profit, and share financial information and responsibility with your employees. If you're an employee, you might advocate for more transparency regarding compensation or how the company is spending its profits.

* * *

If you're inspired to find examples of Positive Money of your own, I encourage you to start by reflecting on a recent financial decision or interaction. What felt positive versus negative about it? What made the difference? Was it what you brought to it or what others did? If you can't think of a recent example, consider one that resonates from deeper in your past or perhaps in the media. Maybe it will show up in a store you frequent or the products you buy. Take time to sit with feelings as well as thoughts, and try to take notes without judgment.

Soon enough, Positive Money will influence how you earn, spend, save, and give. If you're so moved, I'd love to hear about your examples. Let me know if I can share, so we can spread the wisdom together. In the meantime, let's dig into the 7 Principles of Positive Money.

---

1. https://inequality.org/facts/income-inequality/
2. Olen, Helaine, and Pollack, Harold. *The Index Card: Why Personal Finance Doesn't Have to be Complicated*. New York: Penguin Group, 2017.
3. https://oportun.com/financial-education/how-much-debt-does-the-average-american-have/
4. https://www.newyorkfed.org/newsevents/news/research/2022/20220510
5. https://www.bankrate.com/pdfs/pr/20220119-january-fsp.pdf

6. https://www.federalreserve.gov/releases/g19/HIST/cc_hist_memo_levels.html
7. https://gflec.org/wp-content/uploads/2022/04/TIAA-Institute-GFLEC-2022-Personal-Finance-P-Fin-Index.pdf
8. https://www.takechargeamerica.org/the-many-downsides-of-being-unbanked/
9. Olen, Helaine. *Pound Foolish: Exposing the Dark Side of the Personal Finance Industry.* New York: Penguin Group, 2013.
10. Lally, Tammy. *Money Detox.* Florida: Little Lindsey Press, 2018.
11. https://inequality.org/facts/income-inequality/
12. https://www.washingtonpost.com/business/2022/08/25/federal-reserve-jackson-hole-inflation/

Part Two

The 7 Principles

In Part II, you learn about the 7 Principles of Positive Money and how each can be applied.

Positive Money is…

1. **A choice.** *When you choose Positive Money, you choose a relationship with money driven by love rather than fear.*
2. **Generational.** *When you're aware of the beliefs and behaviors you inherit and pass along, you're more intentional about your actions today.*
3. **Serves a higher good.** *When you're grounded by a higher good, you have the interests and needs of others in mind.*
4. **Aligns head, heart, and habit.** *When your thoughts, feelings, and actions related to money are aligned, you experience ease and flow.*
5. **An act of giving and receiving.** *When you give and receive equally, you experience the power of connection.*

6. **Causes no harm.** *When you understand how your money choices cause harm to yourself and others, you take action to mitigate that harm.*
7. **A practice.** *When you practice Positive Money, you apply the principles to daily financial decisions with mindfulness and compassion.*

Principle 1

Positive Money is a choice

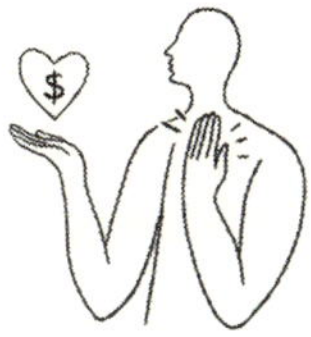

When you choose Positive Money, you choose a relationship with money driven by love rather than fear.

* * *

This first principle of Positive Money is about the power and the will to choose what you want for your relationship with money. When you make the choice, you commit to coming from a place of generosity toward yourself and others in all dimensions of earning, saving, spending, and giving. You aim to take control and assume responsibility for money whenever possible, and you give yourself grace whenever you fall short. Whether the results go up or down, your commitment remains steady.

When you choose Positive Money, you give yourself the gift of intentionality – of deciding how you want to BE in your relationship with money moment by moment, day by day, dime by dime. If you want to be less stressed about it, you ask yourself what less stress looks or feels like. If you want to come from a place of love rather than fear, how might you do that?

> *Just one small positive thought in the morning can change your whole day.* - Dalai Lama

Julie

When Julie's three kids were in elementary school, she would take them to the local toy store to buy a gift or as an activity to get out of the house. She would tell them ahead of time that they could each buy only one thing for themselves and that it had to be under a certain dollar amount. In the store, the experience tended to veer from the plan. Her kids – being kids – were persistent about wanting more than was agreed upon, and she would cave in order to avoid a scene. Afterward, Julie felt frustrated with herself for not sticking to her plan. She also worried about being a bad role model.

* * *

Talk about a true test of parenting! Despite her best intentions, Julie struggled to stick with the plan and then felt bad for falling short. She knew she shouldn't budge on her boundaries but was not up for another temper tantrum from her youngest. She would vow that next time would be different.

I can relate to Julie's story as I imagine many other parents can. We have the best of intentions and then reality hits. Toy stores can be especially challenging because we like to see our children happy. Our inner child shows up, and pretty soon we're all lost in the lego aisle. Like Julie, I would aspire to spend only a certain amount but that aspiration would fly out the window once in the store. It wasn't that we spent lots of money. If anything, I leaned toward sales or being frugal. If we walked away with more than we bargained for, it was likely because of a deal or because we determined together that a game or toy was well worth the expenditure.

The Power of Choice

Julie's story reminds us that our relationship with money can add to the messy experience of parenting. We want to do the right thing – or what we believe is the right thing – and then fall into old habits because we're tired or worn down or don't know what to do.

This is where the power of choice comes in. When you choose Positive Money, you decide that your relationship with money comes from a place of love rather than fear, no matter what others do or say. Even though it can seem difficult to pivot in the moment – even in the midst of chasing children in a toy store – you can pause to ask yourself what love looks like toward yourself and others and which Positive Money principle resonates. You can get curious about what's going on without judgment, and exercise more empathy for yourself or others. You can get honest with yourself about where you're giving in versus what you need to let go.

Your rich life is up to you. It's your choice. If you want to let others decide what that life looks and feels like, then you're still making a decision, albeit one that forfeits that choice.

* * *

Coaching for Julie

Coaching Julie around the first principle of Positive Money I would:

1. Ask her to reflect on her experience, paying attention to her thoughts and feelings. Where did you go off track and how did that feel? What story are you telling yourself about the experience? (Check out the money stories exercise in Part III.) How would you rather feel or behave

in the situation? What thought or action would make you feel different?

2. Capture common themes or patterns and write them down. When you write something down, it lives outside your head—it's there on the page (or screen), staring back at you and keeping you accountable.
3. In this instance, what does Positive Money look like exactly? Teaching kids to be bargain hunters? Modeling alignment between actions and values?

* * *

Once Julie chooses how she shows up in her relationship with money, she can look for and create opportunities for learning and growth. She might decide that beating herself up isn't productive or in the spirit of Positive Money. Then she may explore how she could be more proactive and less reactive. This might incentivize her to examine the language she uses and how she communicates with her loved ones. She might even share her learning journey with her family, so they too can reflect on the consequences of their choices and what they would do again in the same situation.

Often, it's better to learn lessons about money the hard way and when younger. If Julie gave her kids more control over their choices and didn't step in to monitor or judge those choices, what might they learn?

The authors of *The Self-Driven Child* came to support this practice after noticing in their individual practices that even high-performing kids were coming to them acutely stressed and lacking motivation.[1] They learned through their research that the best way to combat stress is to feel more in control of one's life. Though this seems obvious, many parents find it difficult to navigate a hands-off approach, especially as the world seems increasingly unsafe or our need for control gets in the way.

The same goes for adults. Clear values, boundaries, and expectations help us feel safe. When they're clearly communicated, it's easier to make choices and manage others' reactions. For example, had Julie set and kept a boundary like only one toy priced at $20 or less or giving them $20 and telling them to meet her at the checkout when they were ready, she would feel better equipped for the pushback or negotiation she might expect and more aware of the behavior she hopes to model.

Let's be clear. Even with the best of intentions, things can go awry. This is why I prefer principles over directions for guiding actions. *When you choose Positive Money, you're choosing love over fear as the principle behind making financial decisions.* This means you're willing to learn from your mistakes and find the gifts and opportunities in most situations. As Blaire tells us in the following story, "*If we're breathing, we have options.*"

Blaire

Blaire is a certified life coach, event leader, and founder of the Lonewolf District, a community of people learning to love themselves and be accountable for their growth and healing journeys. When I asked her where the Lonewolf name came from, she said, "A lot of pain, a lot of traumas, a lot of loss. I never really felt like I fit in."

Blaire grew up and lives in Baltimore County, Maryland, where she describes her life as abundant and nurturing. She likes to visit her "Street Angels," as she calls them – individuals who are unhoused in the city of Baltimore and who welcome her company and caring that comes from her own place of feeling unseen and not belonging. "I'm half Black, half white, half gay, half straight, half Jewish, half Catholic. I was always too Black for the white kids, but not Black enough for the Black kids. Same thing with sexual orientation."

Living in the gray area took a toll on Blaire, especially in her early twenties when she was haunted by feelings of unworthiness. "I didn't know how to show kindness to money because I didn't know how to show kindness to myself." At a particularly low point, she found herself living in Philadelphia and working in property management while she earned her event leadership certification. "I was working in this 37-story high-rise condo downtown where at least once a week on my lunch break, I would go up to the roof and just look down and think about how there was nothing stopping me from jumping off." One day, she posted on Facebook that she was "sick and tired of being sick and tired" and vowed to go on her own "personal healing evolution," which included everything in her life, especially her relationship with money.

It was soon after this that Blaire met some angels of her own who took her under their wings and helped her to see how her pain could be a source of healing for herself and others. Soon, she began a morning routine. The day we spoke was the 833rd consecutive day of performing a ritual that includes meditation, journaling, and sitting with her thoughts and feelings without judgment.

"I found a way to become friends with my shadows, listen to them, nurture them, and give them the space they need. Yes, there are and there were a lot of shadows around me, my experiences, and my relationship with money. I've been able to go from, 'I don't deserve to live' to 'everything happens for me.'" She shared how this two-year journey has "completely transformed how I see myself, which then means how I see money. It's been just the coolest thing in the world to be both an active participant and an observer in my own growth journey."

* * *

After Blaire spoke about her transformation, I asked her which of the 7 Principles of Positive Money resonated the most. "I don't think it's fair of you to make me choose one," she replied with a smile. "I've found a way to embody each of them through my own healing journey. However, if I had to choose, I would say the most important was that we have a choice. Simple yet profound and clear and concise for the collective population.

How we show up in any given relationship is a choice. To be in a relationship itself is a choice, whether it's with another human being or something like money. As long as we're alive and breathing, we have options."

As we closed out our interview, I found myself in awe of Blaire's combination of tenacity and grace. We discussed how Positive Money can apply even to her Street Angels. "I make a 45-mile drive to the city every day to hand out food and water and protein bars and to ask how they're doing. Often, I get a cheery disposition and an expression of gratitude for being alive and for seeing me. It helps me to remember that a rich life isn't always about what's in your bank account, as you say. I would argue that it's much more about what's in your heart that makes us rich."

Exercise

If you're reading this and wondering if you need Positive Money, I encourage you to do the following exercise.

Track your thoughts or habits related to money for one day and then answer these questions honestly. Be as detailed as you can, especially in capturing your thoughts. For example, if you think, "I wish this wasn't so expensive," try to identify the specific aspects you object to. No judgment here. These questions are helpful for anyone, no matter how much money you have.

1. *How often do you check on your money? Once a day? Once a week? Why or why not?*
2. *What do you say to yourself when you look at your bank balance or pay a bill? Do you pay some more easily than others? Why?*
3. *Do you have any idea where your money is going or coming from? For example, many of us (including me) have subscribed to so many apps and streaming services that we've forgotten about many of them. Does this matter?*

How did it feel to respond to those questions? How might you feel or act differently if you chose Positive Money? Review some examples below.

* * *

Before: I'm bad with money.

Choice: To have a good relationship with money.

After: I gladly get help where needed to assure my financial health.

* * *

Before: We spend too much on frivolous things.

Choice: To get curious about our spending habits without judgment.

After: Look at spending over the last year and discuss individual and joint priorities with my partner.

* * *

Before: Why ask my boss for a raise? I know what she'll say.

Choice: To ask for a raise during my performance review.

After: Come with evidence of the value I bring to the

company and practice making the request beforehand. If I don't get a raise or other benefits I feel are deserved, I'll know I did my best and feel more confident and empowered to advocate for myself.

---

1. Stixrud, William, Ph.D. and Johnson, Ned. *The Self-Driven Child: The Science and Sense of Giving Your Kids More Control Over Their Lives.* Penguin Books, 2019.

Principle 2

Positive Money is generational

When you're aware of the beliefs and behaviors related to money that you inherit and pass along, you're more intentional about your actions today.

* * *

The second principle of Positive Money focuses on what we learned about money growing up and the beliefs and behaviors we pass along to future generations. This is a topic of great interest, as we know from the abundance of movies, books, and television shows that portray the drama around money passing through family systems. *House of Gucci* or *Succession* come to mind. Though these stories can seem extreme, we know that dynamics around inheritance and legacy are particularly treacherous.

When you consider what you've inherited and could pass along from your relationship with money, you might find old patterns of thinking or behaving that no longer serve you or others. For example, let's say you or your family is of the mindset that money is bad or that people with a lot of money are circumspect. Is that a fact or a belief? If a fact, how are you finding evidence and what criteria are you using to test validity? Is your thinking generalized or specific? If a belief, what price are you paying for holding onto this belief?

> *Once you carry your own water, you will learn the value of every drop.* - African Proverb

Ally

Ally grew up in a comfortable suburban community. She was the middle of three children. Both parents had jobs, though her mom worked part-time. Ally had everything she needed or wanted despite how much her parents argued about money. When Ally turned 15, her father got a new job where he earned much more than he had previously. He bought a new car and took everyone on a cruise. Ally's mom stopped working, and her dad was away more often on business trips. Even with these developments, the fighting about money didn't stop. Sometimes, her mom would buy things and tell the kids not to tell their dad about it. Ally was worried that they would get a divorce as had the parents of several of her friends. She also felt uncomfortable when her friends asked if she was rich.

* * *

Ally's story can be read as a tale of achieving the American Dream. Her parents worked hard, made a good life for their family, and enjoyed the spoils of success. More money meant more choices and opportunities and, one would guess, an easing of stress. As we learn from Ally's experience, however, the change in financial status didn't stop the fighting between her parents. No wonder Ally was confused. Was it too little money that caused stress or too much? Should she talk about it with her parents or leave it be? She appreciated the happy times on vacations and getting new things but was also embarrassed when her dad would boast in front of her friends.

Perhaps you can relate to Ally or know someone in her situation. We don't know why her parents argued about money nor what Ally and her siblings picked up from those dynamics. What we do know is that despite the improvements in her family's financial standing, the tensions around money didn't go away. We can also gather that talking about money was not a common practice and that the kids learned that it was ok to keep secrets – in this case around spending. We can also hear that Ally is uncomfortable about being asked if her family is rich. This discomfort could derive from genuine confusion or the fear of being judged.

I can relate to Ally because I grew up with a rich life but had no idea of how others were judging us until I developed class consciousness. Later, I would realize how sensitive my mom was about drawing attention to our abundance as she wrote in the letter I shared at the beginning of the book. Though I wasn't aware of many arguments my parents had about money, I got the message that talking about money was not welcome. I now see this as more of generational behavior than a failure of parenting. In fact, my parents did an outstanding job of cultivating the skills of creative thinking and taking action to do what we were called to do in the world, and I am forever grateful for that. I inherited the values they learned and practiced, and now it's up to me to consider what and how I'm passing them along.

The Power of Generational Awareness

Like Ally and me, you have inherited and will pass along beliefs and behaviors related to money, whether you pay attention or not. If you have a one-size-fits-all attitude that money is bad or that you do everything right while others do everything wrong, then this mindset will likely get passed along or be tied to your legacy. Even if you justify your behavior, one would wonder if it would suit the next generation or do more harm than good. In some cases, when you aren't aware of the impact, you might learn the hard way.

This happened to a nonprofit leader I worked with in a workshop on money mindset. She runs a food pantry and recently had issues with staff stealing inventory. During the workshop, we explored early childhood memories around money. She shared that in her early teens, she had gotten into a summer program that she was excited about until the director told her she no longer qualified because her family income was just above the poverty line. Only those below the poverty line were allowed in the program. She was shocked. She had no idea there was such a line or that her family lived so close to it. Later, she found out that her mother would fill cupboards with empty boxes to make it look like they had more than they did. Through our conversation, she wondered if the pain of discovering the truth about her family finances had anything to do with her ignoring what was really going on behind the closed doors of her warehouse.

As you step back and consider the factors that influence your current financial status and behavior, keep in mind that generational wealth is also influenced by socioeconomic factors such as racial inequality and bias. These barriers to wealth are important to notice, understand, and address where possible. Consider that deliberate acts, such as paying reparations, can serve as our acknowledgment of how privilege plays into our success and can be used for positive change.

The story of Yvon Chouinard, the founder of Patagonia, the outdoor equipment and clothing company, presents another fine example. In 2022, Chouinard and his team decided that instead of going public it was time to "go purpose" by declaring earth as their only stakeholder. He and his family donated the company to a trust with the understanding that all profits moving forward will be dedicated to saving the planet. For Chouinard, generational awareness means taking a bold stand to improve the likelihood we have future generations at all.

Coaching for Ally

Coaching Ally around the second principle of Positive Money I would:

1. Invite her to describe her relationship with money as it is today and as she hopes it will be in the future.
2. Once she paints an image of her future relationship, we might explore the gaps by looking at what she can learn from her past that can help her navigate the future. What does she need to let go of, and what does she need to embrace?
3. If she struggles with answers, I might ask her to consider what her elder, wiser self would advise and what she needs to believe to follow that advice.

If Ally found that these questions brought up uncomfortable emotions and feelings, I would encourage her to practice empathy for herself and others, including her parents, and to understand that blaming money is not where her energies are best directed.

I would also share with Ally specific differences in how generations relate to money. For example, I've seen the struggles of those who inherit wealth that their parents worked so hard to achieve. It's not uncommon for those with an inheritance to feel guilty, hide their wealth, or give it away.

In other instances, they might hang onto it with allegiance that doesn't make sense financially. For example, my grandparents gifted us stock from a major U.S. corporation when we were young. I never sold it because I was focused on it being a gift and, unconsciously, didn't want to let go of that link to the past. As a result, it lost value and was ultimately sold at a loss.

Wherever you are in your money journey, getting curious about your past can offer insights into where you are today and what you want for your future. By doing this exercise, you may be surprised by the greater understanding and deeper appreciation you gain for those who came before you. In my case, I've thought a lot about how Mom was raised by a single mother during the Great Depression and Second World War and how hard it must have been for her to ask for more than basic needs. No wonder she was an expert on being resourceful!

Susie

Susie lives in Colorado and is an artist. She has three grown sons and one grandchild and is building tiny homes on her property she can rent out for recurring income. Her plan is to add a studio on the property for doing her art, hosting workshops or retreats, and enjoying visits from family and friends.

Susie came to me because she realized how much her relationship with money had caused her pain and suffering over the years. It started with her being born. At the time, her mother had just discovered her husband's infidelity and was distraught. She either ignored Susie or was unable to love her. As Susie says, "I was swaddled in rage."

Throughout her childhood, Susie coped with feeling disconnected or unloved by retreating into her art and imagination. Her father remarried a woman Susie describes as emotionally dissociated because of how she treated Susie when she would visit. "She told me straight up that I would never have or belong to the affluent lifestyle that she, my father, and their son lived."

When Susie was in her early 20s, she met the man who would become the father of her three beautiful boys. He was charming, attractive, ambitious, and, at 6'4", he towered over Susie, a 5' bundle of energy and dedication to family. They lived in the lap of luxury with a private plane, fancy cars, and decadence that included his consump-

tion of cocaine and alcohol on a regular basis. Susie played the part of the beautiful and friendly wife focused on raising the kids, all the while hiding how deeply she struggled with her husband's out-of-control addiction.

Unfortunately, when the boys were still young, her husband was indicted for fraud and embezzlement. As she watched her family and their finances fall apart within days, she had no idea of the extent of his wrongdoings and felt abandoned once again by those she trusted.

In the coming days, weeks, and months, Susie was forced to sign away their leveraged assets and come up with a way to support herself and her three boys. Though traumatized by the events, she got scrappy and figured she could rent rooms in their house if she and the boys slept in the primary bedroom. It was this move and selling her art that got her back on her feet and eventually stabilized. Susie's husband went to prison, never fully recovered from his addiction, and died a few years after his release. Susie was truly on her own.

* * *

Susie's story is both heartbreaking and inspiring. Her journey pushed her to look at her relationship with money and to appreciate the power it had to give and take away. By revisiting her childhood, she was able to see how broken her family was and how little it had to do with her. She began to appreciate how she'd coped with difficult times as a child by taking refuge in her art, and she recognized how those talents served her later in life. By building small homes, she not only created a reliable income stream but also the stability she'd yearned for throughout her life.

Today, Susie values family connection more than anything and is proud of her sons and who they've grown up to be. It's been a joy to witness her reconnection to money as a partner and a friend she can count on to show up for her when she shows up for it. As she figures out what that give-and-take looks like and she gains trust in that relationship, I expect positive outcomes for her.

Exercise

To put this principle to work, I suggest you put on your detective hat and look at any evidence you can find that can help you sort fact from fiction. Try answering the following questions:

1. *How might reflection on the past and hope for the future influence your financial decisions and actions today?*
2. *When you listen to your memories, who's talking? What's being said?*
3. *Where do you want your money to flow, and what matters about where it's been spent and invested? How might you steer the narrative in a way that produces a different outcome?*
4. *If you were always told that you need to work hard for your money, what might it look like to work less and earn more or cut back in order to spend more quality time with your family?*

How did it feel to respond to those questions? How might you feel or act differently if you chose Positive Money? Review the examples below.

* * *

Before: I work hard to support our family but feel taken for granted.

Choice: I enjoy supporting my family because family security is important to me.

After: I will do what I can to support my family and ask for the support I need when it becomes too much.

* * *

Before: I'm ashamed of my privilege.

Choice: I'm grateful for my privilege.

After: I will explore ways to use my privilege for good and leave guilt at the door.

* * *

Before: Money doesn't grow on trees.

Choice: Money is like a tree – it grows where it has what it needs.

After: Find ways to grow my money that align with my values.

Principle 3

Positive Money serves a higher good

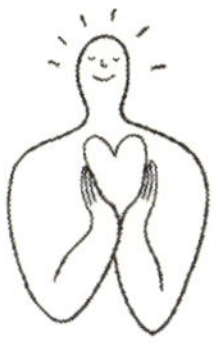

When you're grounded by a higher good, you have the interests and needs of others in mind.

* * *

The third principle of Positive Money reminds us that making financial decisions that are grounded in a higher good or purpose aligns us with our values and helps us focus on the intent and impact of our decisions. It gives us a context and compass to orient us when we earn, spend, save, and give our money. At first, you might think this principle is about charitable giving, fulfilling social responsibilities, or acting according to religious or spiritual beliefs. Surely, these are important and relevant. This principle reaches deeper than that, however. It taps into what matters most at the moment. Often, this is a question of short- versus long-term satisfaction. I want a treat right now. A higher good reminds me that what I *really* want or need is a break or acknowledgement of my efforts.

If you want to live a rich life, this principle is an essential ingredient, and yet it often falls by the wayside. You know it's lacking when no matter how hard you work or try to be good, you don't feel good. Something is still missing even though you're doing "all the things" that are expected of you. This slow and unconscious trading of our true selves for one fashioned by the world around us may explain why even the wealthiest of individuals can feel unsatisfied and disillusioned. In *The Way of Integrity*, author Martha Beck reminds us that our true selves seek simple things like laughing and fresh flowers which are two of my favorites. Once we start craving what others tell us we should desire, we can become blind to our own predilections.[1]

This is where tapping into a higher good – whatever that is for you at the moment – can help zone in on what you really need or want. For example, you're feeling burned out at work and need a break. You think a fancy coffee will help, but take a moment to tune into your body. What do you really need? What would serve a higher or greater good right now? What would truly be of service to you and others? Rescheduling your day? Taking a brisk walk with a friend? Grabbing a 10-minute nap? Your answer might not only make you feel better, but it might also be better for your bank account.

> *You are never too small to make a difference.* - Greta Thunberg

Sam and Julie

When Sam and her partner Julie decided to live together and potentially get married, they had one topic that was particularly challenging to navigate – money. Sam was a steady earner and good with staying within a budget while Julie had college debt and tended to bounce from job to job. Sam wanted to be supportive and enjoyed Julie's creativity and joyful personality but was worried about security. When the topic of money came up, the conversation would often break down.

Both would get defensive and leave the conversation without resolution.

* * *

Sam and Julie's story is not uncommon, especially given that couples can be drawn together because of different strengths or qualities. In this case, Sam has a reliable income and a steady focus on paying monthly bills. Julie may not be as financially reliable, but she clearly brings other qualities to the table. Without the skills or will to talk through their different money styles, however, they may miss a big opportunity for growing together and using their joint strengths to find solutions that work for both of them.

I can relate to Sam's story. I'm more like Julie, and my wife is more like Sam. Early in our lives together, we would struggle to have productive conversations about money because we have such different styles. At first, I judged myself for not being "good with money" but later realized that it was more specifically about fear of taking risks and difficulty with spending money – both comfortable activities for my wife. I've since overcome much of that fear and am getting more comfortable with money flowing through our lives. Without looking at the reasons behind our behaviors, however, we may never have been able to address the issues.

The Power of a Higher Good

If Sam and Julie were able to identify a higher good for their financial relationship, they might find common ground. For example, if they both agreed that they want to be financially fit as individuals and as a couple, they could explore what that looks and feels like in both scenarios. Sam might need something different than what Julie needs. As a couple, they may need something altogether different and can think creatively about what that looks like.

Chances are, compromise and flexibility show up in the mix as well as setting clear boundaries. For example, Sam might agree to be responsible for monthly bills like rent and utilities while Julie handles the food and entertainment. In the process of working it out, they keep asking how their money is serving their higher good.

Coaching for Sam and Julie

Coaching Sam and Julie around the third principle of Positive Money I would:

1. Ask each to share two or three of their core values and then find examples of how this plays out in their relationship. If Sam shares that saving the environment is important to her, I would invite Julie to describe all the ways she appreciates Sam living that value. We would then switch.
2. After each share, I might invite them to recall ways they've supported one another in living their values in the past. What worked? What was appreciated the most? How did supporting one another feel?
3. With those feelings in the air, I would ask them to brainstorm ways they could mutually support one another in bigger endeavors such as planning a wedding or buying a house. The focus would remain on the higher purpose or good – on what joins them together.

As you may gather from the coaching process, the focus is on shared goals and appreciating what each brings to the table. This way, the conversation steers clear of the shame and blame that can derail open communication. That said, both parties need to be willing to participate on equal ground and take responsibility for their actions. If Sam gets frustrated with Julie and decides that she'll never change, then it's up to Sam to decide if she is willing to live with that prospect.

Yvon

Yvon Chouinard is the founder of Patagonia, an outdoor clothing and equipment company valued in 2022 at about $3 billion. The company has always been known for being socially and environmentally conscious, and so when Chouinard decided to retire, he announced that he was giving his company away rather than selling it or taking it public. He and his family wanted a solution that would dedicate future proceeds to combat climate change and protect undeveloped land around the world in the belief that the environment is the ultimate stakeholder.

The Chouinards have had a home in Jackson Hole for years and knew my parents in the small community of longtime residents drawn to the mountains. The Tetons were among the many places he climbed and tested his latest innovations in climbing equipment. Though he claims to have never wanted to be a businessman or own a company, his efforts revolutionized rock climbing and created a brand celebrated worldwide. He also established 1% for the Planet, a call for businesses to commit one percent of annual sales to the environment.

When interviewed about the decision to give the company away, he said, "Hopefully this will influence a new form of capitalism that doesn't end up with a few rich people and a bunch of poor people. We are going to give away the maximum amount of money to people who are actively working on saving this planet."[2]

I have the utmost regard for Chouinard, who shows us what's possible when we're willing to do business a little differently or wear our values on our sleeve. I also agree that, as consumers, we must pay attention to the impact of our buying choices and behaviors and do what we can to mitigate those impacts. Patagonia is leading the way. Now it's up to others to follow.

Exercise

Think of a higher good you connect with. Maybe it's something as broad as protecting the environment or more specific like helping a family member in a time of need. Maybe it's your financial health. If it's not immediately clear, think about what you value like friends or pets. Now that you have some ideas in mind, answer the following questions.

- *What are two or three ways you already earn, spend, save, or give with this higher good in mind?*
- *How does it feel when your money serves a higher good?*
- *What would you change, if anything?*

How did it feel to respond to those questions? How might you feel or act differently if you chose Positive Money? Review the examples below.

* * *

Before: My friend spends too much on silly things.

Choice: To have good relationships.

After: Ask my friend about what drives her spending habits and be present without judgment.

* * *

Before: My kids have no idea how financially strapped we are.

Choice: To educate the kids about finances.

After: Find books and online resources that help them understand how money works and then sit down as a family and share how our family values help us decide how we make financial decisions.

* * *

Before: I need to make more money to measure up.

Choice: I measure up no matter how much money I make.

After: I focus on what matters most to me and celebrate accomplishments.

---

1. Beck, Martha. *The Way of Integrity*: Finding the Path to Your True Self. London: Little Brown, 2021.
2. https://www.nytimes.com/2022/09/14/climate/patagonia-climate-philanthropy-chouinard.html

Principle 4

Positive Money aligns head, heart, and habit

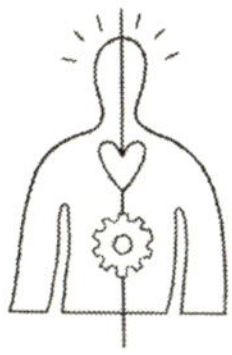

When your thoughts, feelings, and actions related to money are aligned, you experience greater ease and flow.

* * *

The fourth principle of Positive Money reminds us that our beliefs, behaviors, and emotions drive our relationship with money and vice versa. When these three factors are out of alignment, you experience emotions such as guilt or fear or notice behaviors that are not serving you. A simple example is when you make a purchase you don't want to tell others about. Whether this is an exception or a rule, something about the situation feels negative. On the contrary, when the three factors align, you experience greater ease and flow that feels positive or natural. The goal is to learn what both look and feel like for you and to develop the skills and sensitivities to come back to center.

Clients often tell me that this principle is one of the most powerful, and I agree. I use the terms 'Head,' 'Heart,' and 'Habit' as an easy way to remember the three factors. I like to think of them as forming a vertical axis through my body that represents my true self, much like the geographic or magnetic meridians represent the connection between true north and south. If something feels in violation of this true self or out of alignment with what feels right and positive, it's worth looking at.

> *Happiness is when what you think, what you say, and what you do are in harmony.* - Gandhi

Penny

When Penny started her wellness coaching business, she was excited about having more control over her time, the opportunity to be financially independent, and the chance to serve those in need of her services. She worked hard to do "all the things" to grow her business and was committed to doing as much as she could herself because she had the skills but not a lot of money to hire outside help. Unfortunately, sales felt uncomfortable – even slimy – to Penny. Pricing her services was difficult, and she often second-guessed her offers or would undersell her services. The result was that she struggled financially and she felt like a failure.

* * *

Penny's experience describes that of many entrepreneurs when it comes to sales, pricing, and growing their businesses financially. Like Penny, we can be passionate about something we know well and see a need for. We tire of working for others and want to make more of an impact. We figure if we build it, people will come, so we jump in with high hopes and best-laid plans. Unfortunately, about 20% of U.S. small businesses fail within the first year. By the end of their fifth year, roughly 50% are suffering. After 10 years, only around a third of businesses have survived.[1]

The question is why? Though there can be many reasons, I would argue that a major one is our relationship with money. For example, if Penny was thinking that asking others for money is an imposition or creates a burden, it would make sense that she avoids making those requests. (This is called 'getting into other people's pocketbooks.') If she wasn't checking her bank balance or sending invoices frequently enough, this could be a habit stemming from a lack of confidence in her financial knowledge or skills, an aversion to risk, or a combination of both. She also may have felt that reminding people to pay her was pushy or needy.

The Power of Alignment

The impact of being out of sync with how you think, feel, and act in your relationship with money can show up in a variety of ways. An obvious and extreme example is gambling. If you gamble habitually, you might convince yourself it's all good when, in reality, you have an addiction. Less extreme examples are when you feel pressured to pay for something that doesn't sit right, or you feel guilty about having money, so you give it away even if it means financial hardship.

When you apply the fourth principle, you notice when a financial decision or transaction throws you off or doesn't feel right. For example, do you buy things and then hide them from others or judge certain people for their financial choices? Have you ever felt taken advantage of financially or had an experience where what you purchased didn't meet expectations? This happened to me on a trip recently when I needed to grab dinner at the hotel where we were staying. There were few options, and the prices were higher than I was used to paying, but I ordered anyway. The meal was delivered in a big plastic container, not very tasty, and comprised of items that would cost less than ten dollars if purchased at the grocery store. On top of feeling unsatisfied and overcharged for a subpar meal, I felt bad about the environmental waste. The cost was far greater than the gain and a sure sign that this was not a Positive Money moment for me.

If you're judging my response, you're likely tapping into your own set of criteria for making financial decisions, which is exactly what I hope you do. There's no right or wrong here. Rather, it's about noticing where you judge or feel judged and why. In the case of my meal experience, it ran counter to my values of caring about the environment and eating well, so I judged the restaurant for not meeting my needs and myself for not being more careful in my ordering. Had I wanted to turn the experience into a Positive Money moment, I could have shared my experience with the hotel staff in a constructive manner and made a note to clarify expectations next time.

Coaching for Penny

Coaching Penny around the fourth principle of Positive Money I would:

- Ask her to describe a situation that felt challenging to her financially. We would look at how her beliefs and behaviors are driving results and what that feels like.
- After practicing empathy for herself, we would explore options for getting what she needs financially while staying aligned with her values.
- Once she came up with options, I would ask her to put at least one into action and see what happens, reminding her that positive change is a process and can take time but is always worth it.

MaryBeth

MaryBeth describes her relationship with money as originally formed by the push and pull of money dynamics between her parents. Her father was all about saving and thought that spending money on experiences was a waste of money. He made "lots of money" and worked hard for it. Her mother, on the other hand, made less as an art thera-

pist and was all about the value of experiences and living life to the fullest. "My dad made more money and tended to use it for leverage, saying things like, 'I paid for that, so you owe me.'"

Money came at a price. You need to work hard for it. It doesn't come easy. It should be saved and guarded. These are the messages MaryBeth learned from her father and carried into her adulthood and into her business. After about three years of working hard to get clients, she realized she had no idea how to value what she was doing, and the grueling hours didn't scale. She was burned out.

The first step in her transformation was to recognize the need to look inward rather than outward for solutions, so she signed up for a program on manifesting what you want. Through the eight-week program and subsequent coaching, MaryBeth declared that her old money stories had to go. "I honor them as stories, but not as truths." She realized she felt depleted because she wasn't accessing or owning all her assets, including her faith, talent, connection, commitment, and network. She knew they mattered. However, it wasn't until she considered them as part of the package that she was able to embrace her full value and find clients who saw the value of investing in her services.

Now, almost eight years into her business, MaryBeth easily charges 10x the amount she charged for the same service and for several reasons. First, she believes in herself. She believes there's no greater champion for you and the gifts you bring into the world than you. Second, she believes that living your values is your highest form of living a rich life. If you define what this looks like for you, you'll also define the role for money.

Finally, MaryBeth knows it's a process, a journey, and a practice, not something that's 'one and done.' It's putting in the hours, learning by doing, and investing the time.

* * *

When I asked MaryBeth which of the Positive Money principles resonates the most, she said that they all do. However, if she had to pick one, it would be the fourth principle that aligns head, heart, and habit. Given that her expertise is in values, this makes sense. She says that "When we're grounded in what matters most right now, we're closer to the criteria that guide our decisions. It's like having a rudder on the boat, and a sense of the current. We know we're moving ahead and need a source of power and direction. At the same time, we also know that conditions can change, and so we also come prepared to change course whenever needed."

Exercise

Identifying or revisiting your values is a fast and sometimes surprising way to test the alignment between your head, heart, and habits. As MaryBeth reminds us, our values ground us in what matters most right now and what will continue to matter in the foreseeable future. They help us establish boundaries or guardrails so that when we find ourselves in situations that don't feel right, we have insight into why. Let's test this out.

- *What are your core values? (I provide a list of values on my website if you need some ideas.) When I did this recently, I discovered that family security was at the top of the list. This made me review my current priorities and ask myself how I was living that value. As I'm in my mid-60s, it made sense that this would be on my mind and heart.)*
- *Now think about the different ways your value(s) drive how you earn, spend, save, and give and the ways they don't. Notice any gaps or areas of disconnect.*
- *Finally, do a body scan after closing your eyes and taking deep breaths for 2-3 minutes. Do you notice any emotions or feelings coming up and, if so, where in your body? Stay*

curious and take note without judgment. What might these symptoms be telling you about a misalignment between your head, heart, and habits? How might you come back to center?[2]

How did it feel to respond to those questions? How might you feel or act differently if you chose Positive Money? Review the examples below.

* * *

Before: I disagree with my sisters about how to support our aging mother now that our dad has passed, and feel shut out and judged for not caring when I really do care.

Choice: To know we have options (head), show I care (heart), and take action on my commitments (habit).

After: I will practice empathy for myself and others as we go through this challenging time.

* * *

Before: I get anxious about selling. I feel pressure to perform and worry that my customers will be unhappy and say bad things about me.

Choice: Know that money needs to flow to be of service to myself and others (head). I care about my customers and vendors, so when I set up reliable and consistent ways to engage my services, I help everyone thrive. (heart and habit.)

After: Make it easy for my clients to find and access my services.

* * *

Before: I work way too much, so I'm not making time for other things I love or should do.

Choice: To check in on where I'm in or out of alignment in living my values. (heart) If I'm feeling stressed most of the time, I know I need to find ways to come back to center. (habit)

After: I'll be aware of how my strengths can be leveraged for getting back into alignment.

---

1. U.S. Bureau of Labor Statistics in 2020
2. Learn more about somatics at https://en.wikipedia.org/wiki/Somatics

Principle 5

Positive Money is an act of giving and receiving

When you give and receive equally, you experience the power of connection.

* * *

The fifth principle of Positive Money reminds us that when we give and receive equally, we tap into the power of connection to others, to ourselves, and to what matters most in living a rich life. A simple example is when you buy something from an artist whose work you admire and enjoy. You feel good about your purchase because it feels like an equal exchange. The benefit for the artist is that they can continue making art. The benefit to you is that you can appreciate their art whenever or wherever you choose.

I love this principle because most of us give far more easily than we receive. If someone offers us help or wants to give us a gift, we feel awkward, undeserving, or guilty. We worry that we should do or say something in return or that we're being needy, greedy, or somehow broken. For example, if you consider yourself a provider, my guess is that your loved ones find it hard to give you gifts.

Why? You likely learned at an early age to fend for yourself. If you ever needed something, you figured out how to get it. Eventually, you became the provider for others because you're good at it and find it rewarding. This can be healthy as long as you're able to receive support in other ways. It can be unhealthy if you don't accept nonmonetary support easily or think you're responsible for everyone's happiness. When this is the case, you can suffer from burnout or feel resentful if you aren't appreciated.

My wife is a good example of this dynamic. She's the primary provider in our family and loves to give. We call her "Mommy Make It Happen" because she's on top of any need that arises and enjoys being effective. While we're grateful for all she does, it can be challenging to give her gifts or to do things for her as she doesn't ask for much. It can also be hard for her to not feel productive as this is how she feels worthy.

> *Abundance is the expectation and acceptance of ease and flow.* - Deepak Chopra

Jenna

Jenna is 30 years old and single. She is a valued team member at work and often spends evenings and weekends at the office, even when she isn't paid for the overtime. She has always enjoyed working and is often promoted for her work ethic and responsible nature. She loves to save money and watch it grow but has a hard time spending it, especially on herself. Growing up in a family of five meant that money was often tight and her parents worked several jobs to make ends meet. She vowed that when she grew up and had her own family, things would be different.

* * *

Jenna is someone you want on your team at home or at work because she's responsible, caring, and willing to do what it takes to get the job done. She's admired and appreciated for her discipline and dedication to her work and is thought of as successful by her parents and friends. What her friends and family don't know is that she wishes she could work less and enjoy life more. She doesn't like spending her nights and weekends at work but worries that if she doesn't, she'll be judged as disloyal or passed over for promotions. She's also afraid to ask for a raise because she thinks she hasn't done enough to deserve it. She desperately wants to meet a life partner but rarely makes time for that pursuit.

Jenna's story is relatable, especially in times when one job often doesn't cover rising costs of living and employers are cutting back on full benefits. In the midst of such hardships, it's understandable that employees are worried about losing their jobs or holding down several to meet basic needs. In Jenna's case, however, there's more to the story. Jenna is going above and beyond consistently at work but not earning nor asking for more. Though she's appreciated, there's no guarantee of more money or a promotion. Meanwhile, she's missing out on pursuing her dream of having a family.

Jenna's story also brings up common financial challenges for women. Financially, we already earn less than men, and our earning power is often curtailed by our role as parents and caregivers. Though we want to be there for our loved ones, it can mean sacrificing our career aspirations and earning potential in a world that celebrates work and earning more than home and caregiving.

As I noted before, our self-worth is too often connected to our net worth. I know I judged myself as less than my working peers when I didn't have a full-time career. When I look back, I realize that though I was confident in my choices, I still felt caught between being a mom and wanting to prove myself professionally. Had I examined my life more through the lens of the fifth principle of

Positive Money, I may have realized how truly rich my life was by being able to give and receive the benefits of both.

The Power of Giving and Receiving

If you want a rich life, as Jenna does, the fifth principle of Positive Money can help you on your way to one. At the very least, it can draw your attention to how you give and receive and lay bare any imbalances. At the most, it can help you experience the power of deep connection, which is what the cycle of giving and receiving is all about. When you give and receive equally, an exchange of energy is created that can be felt going both ways. This is what money coaches call ease and flow. When money is recognized for what it is – currency whose value is determined by exchange – then finding ways to keep that energy flowing is a good thing for everyone.

That said, not all giving or receiving qualifies as an act of Positive Money. If you attach expectations or conditions to transactions, you can suffer when they aren't met or adhered to. A Positive Money move would be to give money knowing that you may not be paid back, or the terms of the loan are laid out and understood by both parties. You would be dialed into why you're giving in the first place and what you receive in the process.

When you give and receive easily, you're more connected to your core values and what matters most. Money is merely a facilitator in such transactions.

Coaching for Jenna

Coaching Jenna around the fifth principle of Positive Money I would:

- Ask her to create a picture of the life she dreams about in as much detail as possible. I might even take her through

a visualization of what it would feel like to be living that dream.
- Then we would talk about what she needs to make that happen financially, emotionally, and otherwise and how giving and receiving would support the process.
- We might discuss how she could set boundaries for herself at work and how she would handle the consequences if either she or her employer failed to honor them.
- We might also explore the stories she tells herself about earning and saving and how she might start "investing" by revising those stories.

Exercise

If you want to work on building your giving and receiving muscles, I suggest you start with an inventory of how you give and receive outside your relationship with money.

- *Do you give your time and energy freely when others need help?*
- *Do you like being the hero? If so, do you give others the chance to also be the hero? How so?*
- *If you add money into the mix, what changes, if anything?*

Now that you have some examples in mind, how might your beliefs or behaviors be contributing to the outcomes? For example, if you believe that money is toxic, you may be blocking money from coming your way or giving it away out of guilt for having it. If you like being the hero and resist letting others help you, you may be depriving others of the joy of lending a hand. In any of these scenarios, the balance of giving and receiving is off-kilter and therefore throws off an ideal flow of money.

How did it feel to respond to those questions? How might you feel or act differently if you chose Positive Money? Review the examples below.

* * *

Before: When I'm invited to a networking event, I get anxious. I feel so awkward standing around, not knowing what to say even though I know it's important to my business.

Choice: To think of networking as giving to others.

After: I look forward to opportunities where I can learn all the different ways I might be able to help someone.

* * *

Before: I disagree with my boss about spending priorities. She is generally easy to work with but when we discuss the budget we struggle and I don't feel comfortable challenging her.

Choice: Schedule time with my boss to learn more about what goes into making and managing the budget.

After: When I keep an open mind, I receive more information that helps me understand so I can give my support where it matters most.

* * *

Before: My bestie is very needy. She wants to come over a lot and it's often around lunch or dinner. I feel bad about not wanting her over as I have other things going on, and it's doing a number on my food budget.

Choice: Take charge of the time we spend together and the terms of that engagement.

After: I love spending time with my bestie in small doses so I let her know ahead of time when it works for her to come over and what to bring.

Principle 6

Positive Money causes no harm

When you commit to causing no harm in your relationship with money, you aim to understand how your choices cause harm to yourself and others and take action to mitigate that harm.

* * *

The sixth principle of Positive Money helps you recognize how you're capable of inflicting harm on yourself and others in the ways you think, feel, and act in your relationship with money. This can look as simple as buying something that puts you in debt or as complex as ongoing patterns of feeling unworthy. If you use money for control or power over others as a measure of your self-worth or a way to separate yourself from others, it's being used for harm. If you get down on yourself for not earning more or you think you're stupid because you don't know more about money, you're also causing harm.

In Part I, I talk about three ways we can have an unhealthy relationship with money, starting with it being adversarial. Though the harm done may be obvious, the source of that harm is often unclear. A good example is imposter syndrome. Though this condition may seem unrelated to money, it can show up in your financial life as resistance to getting paid what you're worth or thinking that people are paying you merely to be nice or to have pity on you. The fear is that sooner or later you'll be found out as a fraud for failing to meet expectations. The harm can range from not meeting your financial needs to not feeling worthy of living.[1]

When you let others determine your value or worth, you lose sight of the value and worth you offer to others. Though it may be difficult to feel that love for yourself at times, it couldn't be more important that you do so. It's natural to hold yourself to high standards, but you must also accept your vulnerability and imperfection.

> *Although the world is full of suffering, it is also full of the overcoming of it.* - Helen Keller

Tony and Aliyah

Tony and Aliyah have two young children, ages two and four. Both sets of grandparents live nearby and help with the kids. Aliyah's parents were strict with her growing up and are strict with their grandchildren. Tony's family is more outgoing and playful. His parents like to buy gifts for the grandkids, sometimes quite extravagant ones, and don't often check to see if it's ok. Tony and Aliyah are on a tight budget, and Aliyah manages their finances. She thinks his parents spoil their children. Tony disagrees. When Aliyah asks him to talk to his parents about her concerns, he tells her she needs to lighten up or talk directly with her in-laws. Predictably, the kids prefer to hang out with the "fun" grandparents.

* * *

In this scenario, Aliyah feels frustrated about not being heard or supported by her husband around her repeated requests, and she avoids sharing her concerns with her in-laws. Tony feels stuck in the middle, especially when he agrees more with his parents than with his wife. Aliyah knows that she can be uptight, and most of the time appreciates Tony and his family's lighthearted and generous nature. However, she also worries that if she lets her guard down, she'll lose credibility and control, and the kids will grow up thinking they can get anything they want.

Tony and Aliyah's story illustrates how couples can be attracted to one another for their complementary strengths or qualities. Financially, one person's strengths may be in earning while the other's may be in saving or being thrifty. Tony probably relies on Aliyah for her financial diligence while she appreciates his zest for life. Unfortunately, these differences can get amplified when family and other stressors are added to the mix. Conflict can occur, which in and of itself is neither good nor bad. However, it can lead to harm in the absence of conflict management skills or a commitment to address the issues in a healthy way. Without these interventions, we can get worn down and resigned to the status quo.

Take the case of a young woman who worries that her fiance's bad money habits will derail their future marriage. In seeking advice from a popular advice columnist, she shares that her fiance has charged $8K on credit cards she didn't know he had after he promised to pay off other fees and debts. The purchases were for non-essentials and were only disclosed after she confronted him. He felt ashamed but refused help, which is why his partner was asking for advice. The answer was short and to the point, "Leave him. As much as he was bad with money, his refusal to get help was a sign of stubbornness, pride, and inflexibility. All which will make you *miserable.*"[2]

Though the advice was harsh, the story of this young couple shows how we cause harm to ourselves and others when we let pride, fear, or other saboteurs manage our money. For example, when you spend beyond your means, you do harm to your future self by saddling her with debt. When you already have enough income and keep working crazy hours, you may miss out on the rich life you're supposedly working so hard for, or you may face increased health risks like those reported by the World Health Organization. According to its 2021 report, "People working 55 or more hours each week face an estimated 35% higher risk of a stroke and a 17% higher risk of dying from heart disease, compared to people following the widely accepted standard of working 35 to 40 hours in a week."[3]

* * *

In *Overcoming Underearning* Barbara Stanney writes that "Underearners are self-saboteurs who never live up to their earning potential. Ironically, many work incredibly hard. Yet, they are ashamed to admit that money matters to them. They have a high tolerance for low pay."[4]

When I first read Stanney's book, I was both relieved and ashamed. While I was gaining insight into my relationship with money, I was also beating myself up because I saw underearning as a fault or deficiency. In a world where earning more is a sign of success, earning less is a sign of the opposite. In a city like Washington, DC, where we live, status is currency. The first question you get asked when meeting someone new is, "What do you do?" Though an innocent question, it can trigger an identity crisis for some, including the parent who's been home all day changing diapers.

Another way you can harm yourself financially is when you habitually spend beyond your means. The term for this is 'overspending,' which can be driven by unmet emotional needs. Potential impacts are going into debt, hiding purchases from loved ones, as in the case of the fiance above, and wasting resources, as when goods are needlessly bought, returned, or discarded.

The Power of No Harm

When you commit to the sixth principle of Positive Money, you get curious about the subtle or not-so-subtle ways your words or actions may cause harm and you aim to make changes that will lead to more positive outcomes. The following are some examples.

- **Notice the words or phrases you use when talking about money that might be hiding your bias or making it ok for you to judge.** For example, if you automatically say something is 'expensive,' is that a fact or your opinion? A fact would be that the price for a Mercedes is higher than that of a Kia. Your opinion may be that the Mercedes is expensive while someone else might not describe it that way. If you want to stick with the facts, the Mercedes is outside your price range right now, though perhaps it won't be one day. While you reflect on how or when you use the word "expensive," think about other ways you attach judgment to everyday words like 'rich,' 'poor,' or 'lazy.'

- **Replace old stories or habits that no longer serve you with ones that do.** When one of my business clients realized how often she assumed what her customers could or could not afford, she decided that it was time to stay out of their pocketbook and focus more on hers. She thought about different offers she could make that felt good for her and her bank account, knowing that some potential clients would accept and others wouldn't.

- **Accept that others may not agree with you or adhere to your worldview.** This can be a tough one, especially when you're so certain about your beliefs and values that you judge others for theirs. For example, I'm worried about the impacts of climate change and can't believe that millions of others aren't either because they don't know or don't care. This causes me pain because I worry about our future and feel so helpless. I do have options, however. I can help to educate and advocate.

Coaching for Tony and Aliyah

A starting point for any client is to know what you can and can't control, making room to listen for and process the shame that can arise when admitting faults or shortcomings. For Tony and Aliyah, I would ask each to identify the strengths they bring to the table and to acknowledge how those strengths serve their relationship and family.

We might even go back to why they fell in love in the first place to move them from a defensive mode to an appreciative one. From there, I might invite them to reflect on how their behavior is causing harm, whether to themselves or others, and how they might find empathy for their younger selves.

During our coaching session, I might remind them that early childhood experiences, especially negative ones, can make it hard to trust and change as an adult. As psychologist Jonathan Haidt writes, "The mind reacts to bad things more quickly, strongly and persistently than to equivalent good things."[5]

In various studies including one done by relationship experts, it can take five positive interactions to counter one negative one.[6]This is why I like to teach simple and effective ways to build and maintain mental fitness and why Positive Money is a practice. We need to keep helping our brains to create new neural pathways so we have more control over our responses.

Exercise

The first step in applying the sixth principle of Positive Money is to take a quick back-of-the-napkin inventory of where you might be doing harm to yourself in your words or actions. For example, do you:

- *Avoid looking at your bank account out of fear of what you'll find?*
- *Get angry at your kids for wanting to buy something you can't afford?*
- *Blame your partner for the financial situation you're in?*
- *Aim to please others to the point that you don't advocate for your needs?*
- *Work so hard that you lose touch with loved ones?*

If you answered yes to any of these questions, chances are that fear is in control, or at least your saboteurs are at work. What does it look or feel like when they're in control? What would it look or feel like if they weren't? What wisdom might your elder, wiser self offer?

* * *

How did it feel to respond to those questions? How might you feel or act differently if you chose Positive Money? Review the examples below.

Before: I'm angry with myself for not putting six months of savings away, especially as the economy is so uncertain. Now I have to borrow from my family and I'm so embarrassed.

Choice: To not beat myself up and, instead, practice

self-care so I can face the uncertainty ahead with more grace and compassion.

After: Create a payback plan and communicate that to my family. I will also get some help on how to do that if it feels hard because I don't like being in this position.

* * *

Before: A few investments our parents made and gifted to us are in companies whose values I don't agree with.

Choice: To know where and how my money is being spent in ways that I disagree with.

After: Meet with a financial advisor who shares similar values to mine and who can help me to identify and research companies I feel good about.

* * *

Before: I get angry with the kids when they constantly ask for more things. They're ungrateful and it makes me not want to give them anything because they expect it.

Choice: To reflect on how we got here in the first place and what love would look like moving forward.

After: I sat down with each child to listen to how they see the situation and discovered that each had a different story. I shared what it felt like for me and asked how they might react if in my shoes. We agreed to come up with individual action plans that include them earning money to pay for what they want with no judgment from me.

---

1. Financial stress is a serious concern. If you or someone you care about needs help, please reach out to the National Suicide Prevention Lifeline by texting or calling 988 at any time day or night.
2. https://www.washingtonpost.com/advice/2022/12/12/carolyn-hax-debt-fiance-lying/
3. https://www.who.int/news/item/17-05-2021-long-working-hours-increasing-deaths-from-heart-disease-and-stroke-who-ilo#:~:text=The%20study%20concludes%20that%20working,35%2D40%20hours%20a%20week.
4. Stanney, Barbara Stanny. *Overcoming Underearning.* New York: HarperCollins, 2005.
5. https://archive.nytimes.com/dealbook.nytimes.com/2013/06/14/overcoming-your-negativity-bias/?mtrref=undefined&assetType=REGIWALL
6. https://www.gottman.com/blog/the-magic-relationship-ratio-according-science/

Principle 7

Positive Money is a practice

W*hen you practice Positive Money, you apply the principles to daily financial decisions with mindfulness and compassion.*

* * *

The seventh principle of Positive Money focuses on *how* to apply the principles in mindful and compassionate ways. Like most practices, it starts with an interest in or a need for what the practice promises and a commitment to try it out. If you like what you see or feel, especially if it fills a void or speaks to you in a certain way, you're inspired to do more either on your own or with a teacher or community that helps you move toward a practice.

If you've ever started or adopted a practice, this process may sound familiar. When I got serious about yoga in my early forties, I'd already dabbled in it years before and was looking for something physical and spiritual. I decided on Ashtanga yoga, took a few classes, and eventually signed up for a year and went regularly. Little did I know how much that decision and practice would get me through the next 20 years. Those classes were a sanctuary and an opportunity to reflect on what I brought to the mat. Not only was I learning about yoga, but I was learning about myself; how I did or didn't compare myself to others, how I navigated a bad knee, and what it meant to show up.

Today, I'm grateful that my yoga practices sustained me through difficult times and reminds me of how much I rely on mental and physical fitness for my mental health. I can't imagine functioning without it. I wonder if you can relate. What practices do you rely on that keep you grounded and connected? How did they come about? Did a friend invite you to be a running partner and now you count on those runs to do more than build and sustain leg muscle? What about that morning ritual of journaling or praying?

This is why the practice of Positive Money is also the final principle. It's a long game played daily. It's many conversations we have with money, not just one. It's a call to action grounded in the idea that we get more bang for our buck when we invest our buck in something we value.

> *You cannot shake hands with a clenched fist.* - Indira Gandhi

Sarah

Sarah avoids money conversations. They make her feel anxious and embarrassed because she thinks she should know more about finances. At home, she defers the management of household expenses to her partner. When asked about a recent purchase, she gets defensive. At work, she's been encouraged to apply for a more senior position but is afraid that she isn't cut out for it or that her colleagues will learn how unqualified she is. She never learned about managing money growing up because her mom took care of it and her dad wasn't around much. When Sarah asked about money, she was told that she shouldn't worry about it. When she got her first job, she had no idea how to ask about her pay, so she just said yes to whatever was offered.

* * *

Sarah's relationship with money appears to be influenced by fear and self-doubt. She judges herself harshly and assumes others are judging her similarly. As a result, she defers to others or lacks confidence even as others believe she can take on more responsibility. No wonder she's found a money-savvy partner. While she enjoys the support, she's putting herself at risk if she becomes single again since she lacks the knowledge and skills to manage her finances.

Sarah's not alone in avoiding money matters, especially those that bring up insecurities or feelings of discomfort. This avoidance can seem manageable until it catches up to us – sometimes in unexpected or costly ways like a divorce, a fire or hurricane, or a death. I can cite many examples of what this looks like including one in which a good friend passed away suddenly during treatment for an illness she was managing. Neither she nor her husband – both in their 70s – had a will, and neither expected her death so soon. Settling the estate was an additional source of stress for her widower.

Had these friends or Sarah developed a Positive Money practice, they would have been better equipped to understand or address their resistance to money matters. If Sarah were willing to exercise compassion for herself and get curious about why she avoids money conversations, she might discover that her parents' decision to exclude her from money conversations was their way of showing love. Had our friends thought about their money being generational or serving a higher good, they might have thought of their will as a way to pass money along to extended family members and charities.

Thinking of Positive Money as a practice has helped me in similar ways. For example, when I want to put off comparing insurance plans or buying insurance at all (yuck), I take a few moments and think about how buying insurance serves a higher good. Since family security is my highest priority, I consider how grateful I've been to have insurance in times of need. It's like buying a fire extinguisher, generator, or safe in case of an emergency. I don't want to need it, but knowing I have it brings me comfort.

The Power of the Practice

As a reminder, the practice of Positive Money focuses on our head, heart, and habit. In Sarah's case, she gets defensive when asked about her spending. If this happens occasionally, she could chalk it up to being tired or having a boundary crossed. Because it happens consistently, a practice of mental fitness would help Sarah get curious about what's going on and have the skills to come back to what matters most.

* * *

I offer specific ways to build your mental fitness in Chapter 7 under Positive Money practices.

* * *

Coaching for Sarah

Coaching for Sarah would include an invitation to imagine what a Positive Money practice might look like for her. I would give her the list of principles and ask her to choose one that resonates.

For example, if Sarah chose the fourth principle about aligning head, heart, and habit, we might explore what that would look like in action in as much detail as possible. Over the coming days or weeks, we would explore opportunities for her to commit to certain actions and take note of what worked well. We would continue to work in this way, focusing on the positives and helping her learn practices that challenge her thinking and give her tools for navigating moments of discomfort and doubt.

Exercise

- *Think about a recent transaction or encounter that involved money that challenged you. Was it a disagreement with a loved one? Paying a speeding ticket you thought was excessive? Not getting paid on time for work you completed?*
- *Sit with that memory for several minutes and notice the thoughts and feelings that come up. Are there familiar patterns of thinking or behaving? If so, write them down.*
- *Identify questions you ask yourself that gin up negative responses and try to reframe those questions. For example, if you're frustrated by the parking ticket, you might wonder why they charge so much for going only six miles over the speed limit in a school zone. A reframe might be to wonder what it feels like to be a crossing guard who has to manage cars while getting kids across the street safely.*

When I put myself through this exercise recently, I thought about a flight I bought for a trip to surprise a friend. I don't spend money easily and am a bit of a homebody, so doing this was a stretch. I noticed feeling anxious, wondering if I was making a mistake. I also noticed a habit of second-guessing myself. A question that came up was "Will this be worth it?" If I wanted to apply the seventh principle of Positive Money, I could reframe the question to, "What matters most about being there for my friend?" I could also ask myself when I've had similar doubts in the past and found that it was worthwhile to push past them.

* * *

How did it feel to respond to those questions? How might you feel or act differently if you chose Positive Money? Review the examples below.

Before: I was so anxious when we had to buy health care insurance. I was worried we would make the wrong choice and lose money unnecessarily.

Choice: To do some mini-meditations before making a big financial commitment like health care insurance, and take note of my fears.

After: I asked myself how having health care insurance for myself and my family feels, and what I can do to focus on the benefits rather than the costs.

* * *

Before: My husband and I have different relationships with money. He's a spender and I'm a saver. Sometimes he teases me about buying things on sale or using coupons. The kids think I'm a tightwad.

Choice: To set up a money date with my husband so we could talk about this dynamic.

After: During our money date, we set a timer and some guidelines for sharing our different perspectives. It was the beginning of a regular schedule of money dates where we agreed to support one another and show the kids how it's ok to disagree as long as there is mutual respect.

* * *

Before: I avoid looking at my bank account at every cost. I'm afraid of what I'll see and it reminds me of how little I take care of my money.

Choice: To love my money.

After: I scheduled a time after my morning coffee to check my bank balances three times a week. If I miss, I find a question that helps to motivate me like, "What does love look like in this situation?"

Part Three

Positive Money at Work

"There is a gigantic difference between earning a great deal of money and being rich." - Marlene Dietrich

Positive Money makes you feel empowered, engaged, and excited about life. You're choosing Positive Money because you believe in it and appreciate approaching the financial decisions in your life with intention so that you see more positive results.

You learned about Positive Money and why we need it in Part I. In Part II, you learned about the 7 Principles of Positive Money and how to apply each by example. Now, in Part III, you'll learn about different practices and resources and get tips for putting Positive Money to work.

* * *

Before we jump in, I encourage you to recall the examples of Positive Money you already see at work. Did they include a recent interaction you had? A story you heard, an unexpected gift you received, or a simple night out with friends?

What resonated based on everything you've learned so far? What was present? How did it feel to be a witness or a participant? What role did money play?

A standout for me is the television series about Ted Lasso, an American football coach who is hired by a wealthy divorcée to coach the English soccer team AFC Richmond. Everyone wants Ted to lose, including the person who hired him. Despite the adversity he faces, including his demons, his positive energy and unconditional love on and off the field pay off in and out of the locker room. Though the storyline isn't directly about money, I couldn't help but notice the link between his focus on the positive and the team's success.

One of my favorite sources for Positive Money stories is *StoryCorps*, a platform for hosting, preserving, and sharing stories of connections between people. Intimate conversations are recorded all across the country and then edited and shared. They often speak to what mattered most in a lifetime or during a particular time of hardship. In one story, Thompson Williams and his son Kiamichi-tet talk about Thompson's father, a tribal leader with the Caddo Nation in Oklahoma and a World War II veteran. They recall a family Christmas when there was no money left for presents. Kiamichi-tet was 11 years old and his sister, AuNane, was 14. Thompson was a teacher's assistant for students with special needs — work he loved but that didn't pay well. His wife, an artist, sold paintings and handmade Christmas ornaments.

As the holidays approached, Thompson realized that they had used all their funds to pay bills and buy groceries. He'd been offered a job that would pay more money, but that would mean he wouldn't be home with his family or working with the special needs children he loved working with. He decided to take the job so his kids could have Christmas.

When Thompson took his children aside to share his decision, his daughter was quiet for a while and then said, “Dad, your kids need you more than we need presents.” A week later, people started buying his wife’s ornaments, and she ultimately made enough money for gifts so that he could keep the teacher’s assistant job. A modern-day "It's a Wonderful Life" story, the memory of that Williams family Christmas reminds us that contributing to our community can enrich our lives in more ways than one.

Chapter 1

Positive Money for Families

> *I've always put my family first and that's just the way it is.* - Jamie Lee Curtis

A woman in her early 60s shared her present challenge with an online group. She and her husband, both retired, live in a small house. In the past year, their two grown sons have moved back in with them. One has a history of addiction and hasn't been able to hold down a job because of anger issues. The other son moved in with his girlfriend, three dogs, three cats, "huge" debt, and "terrible" credit. She was reaching out for advice.

At first, you might judge this woman for being a pushover or for failing to set boundaries. You might take issue with the sons for taking advantage of their parents, or you may relate to them and feel shame about it. Perhaps you're feeling grateful that you don't have such problems and wonder how you would cope if it was you.

Whatever your perspective, her situation is not unusual even when you take rising costs of living and the lingering effects of the pandemic out of the equation. Her children expect to be supported, and she is providing that support. Chances are that her sons will continue with this expectation even if they feel ashamed about it. Until a party decides they've had enough and takes a different action, the status quo will prevail.

If Positive Money were to be practiced here, family members would ask themselves what a healthy relationship with money would look like for them. At first, they might choose a principle that defends their actions. For example, the mother might say, "Oh yes, it's serving a higher good by providing a roof over their heads during challenging times." In this case, I would counter with, "Yes, that's true. But does it need to be *your* roof?"

As this glimpse into one family's challenge around money demonstrates, money is one of the most difficult or uncomfortable topics for families to address. This is one reason why the second principle of Positive Money is about the generational patterns we inherit and pass along. On one hand, we want to think we're our own person apart from our family. On the other hand, we're cut from the same cloth.

Unfortunately, this push and pull can create tensions, as the story of our 60-year-old mother reminds us. Without the skill and will to address these tensions, a rich life can seem more fantasy than reality. The question is how or where Positive Money can help mitigate tensions and deepen connections so that all can enjoy a rich life, even when we have different ideas of what that looks like.

In this chapter, we'll discover specific ways families can foster a positive relationship with money by looking at how to teach kids about money, how to develop a sense of financial responsibility, and how siblings and couples can support one another.

Kids and Money

As parents or guardians, we want to raise money-smart kids so that they grow up to be happy and secure. We want them to learn about earning, spending, saving, and giving and how to manage their money. We want them to avoid mistakes we made or help take care of us in our later years. These are a few of the many reasons we want them to be financially literate.

Unfortunately, it is often we who are ill-equipped to manage money, much less advise others on how to do so. We also run into disagreements over the best way to handle this vital dimension of parenting.

* * *

Allowance

Agreeing on how to "do" allowance is often where the journey begins. We assume it will be pretty simple and straightforward. Yet, as I learned from my own experience as a parent and then teaching about allowance through my Pizza Money® programs, it's not.

We each think about an allowance differently. For those of us with partners, sometimes our thinking syncs with theirs, and sometimes it doesn't. Throw in the unique personalities and needs of kids and pretty soon what appears easy becomes much more complex.

This is why I came up with four **Allowance Types**. They reflect parents' or guardians' different approaches to the matter. I describe each type below and what it looks like through the lens of Positive Money.

- The **Consultant** wants children to learn about money through trial and error. The focus is on practice and learning. The role of the parent is to serve as a resource should the child reach out for guidance.
- The **Employer** wants children to understand the connections between skills, talent, effort, and earning. The focus is on providing them with practical experiences or jobs that teach them about work. The role of the

parent is to help the child build skills, create opportunities for earning, and process lessons and observations.
- The **Planner** wants children to learn the practice and value of saving and the satisfaction of delayed gratification. The focus is on how to care for money and make it grow. The role of the parent is to help the child learn how money grows, how to set goals and work toward them, and the satisfaction of achieving those goals.
- The **Teacher** wants children to learn about all dimensions of money with the intention of developing their financial literacy. The focus is on how money works. The role of the parent is to teach the child through daily experiences and to provide additional learning opportunities as needed.

You might wonder what happens if there are clashing opinions about which approach is preferable. No worries. The four types are not mutually exclusive; they are complementary. The goal for each parent or guardian is to decide which Allowance Type resonates, choose it as a methodology, apply Positive Money principles, and stay consistent. The aim is for everyone to be clear about the objectives so activities can be planned and expectations managed. If your child learns multiple lessons about money, then all the better.

* * *

How to:

As the Consultant - If your child wants a new bicycle, you might ask them how they propose to earn the money to pay for it. If they get upset and want help, you can remind them that it's a great opportunity to learn how money works. You might also add that you have faith in their ability to figure it out. (This is to choose Positive Money.)

As the Employer - If your child wants to make money, you can assign them specific chores and decide what they would earn for each based on their level of skill and hard work. A Positive Money move would be to talk about the fourth principle, the alignment of head, heart, and habit. When their head and heart are in the game, they'll start to develop habits that are rewarded.

For the Teacher - If you want your child to learn about spending, saving, giving, and earning, you could review the list of principles together and then ask your child to find examples of them in the real world. When they do, discuss the example in detail and then ask if they have experienced anything similar.

For the Planner - If you want your child to learn about saving, you could talk about the principle of giving and receiving as a way of taking care of their future self. You could arrange for them to experience the power of giving and then talk about what it feels like to be generous (what they *get* from the experience). You can also explain how saving helps our money grow, so we can give even more.

Financial Responsibility

One objective in raising money-smart kids is to help them learn what it means to be financially responsible. Think back on a time you went out for pizza with friends. How did you decide who would pay? If you go on vacation with your parents, do you expect them to pay for you even if you can afford it? If you're in a serious partnership, how do you distribute financial responsibilities and how's that going for you?

The saying, "The buck stops here," is a way of clarifying financial responsibility. The "buck" either stops with you, or you pass it along. For example, if you assume your husband will take care of you financially, you could regret it if you get divorced or he becomes unable to support you. In this case, you're passing the buck along by expecting support. Instead, you could have the buck stop with you by being clear about and discussing your responsibilities and agreeing on a system for checking in and accountability. Money Dates, discussed in the next chapter, are ideal for this exercise.

* * *

How do we learn about financial responsibility?

Our relationship with financial responsibility can be traced to our childhood, either through general conditioning or specific events like a parent leaving or losing money you were given in trust. A friend once shared that, as the oldest, she was responsible for her and her younger sibling's lunch money. One day it was stolen out of her backpack. She felt terrible because she wasn't careful enough and they all had to go without lunch. To this day, she remembers that incident and believes it contributes to her financial vigilance.

Many women grow up thinking their Prince Charming will appear, sweep them off their feet, and be their sugar daddy for the rest of their happy lives. This is by no means a judgment. Such expectations can be traced back to cultural norms, media messaging, or both. Men can be saddled with the same expectations of being the provider and suffer when they don't live up to those expectations.

If you grow up without expecting financial support or in a family where financial support was conditional, you may have decided that being financially responsible for everything is ultimately the easiest, safest, and most ethical thing to do. This is often the story of those who start their own businesses or work from a young age. It's not uncommon to hear about someone stepping up as the breadwinner after growing up in a household put at risk because one parent left and failed to pay child support. This expectation of financial responsibility can be hard to lift off the shoulders of those who assume it's up to them to take care of others. Such cases where can lead to burnout and resentment.

For those of us fortunate enough to have financial support growing up, the line between what we're responsible for and what we're not can be a moving target. As parents, we want our kids to be financially responsible adults, and yet we struggle to set and stick to money boundaries such as requiring our teens to pay for their clothes. We think we're being mean, unreasonable, or creating unnecessary hardship for them, especially when we can afford to pick up the bill.

In "*The Opposite of Spoiled,*" Ron Leiber, a personal finance columnist for the New York Times, talks about the new world of money that families are navigating.[1] While we may still want to help our children with a wedding or to buy their first home, that option may no longer be available or puts us in the tough spot of deciding between their needs and our own. Leiber recommends that rather than retreat from this tough conversation or lie about what's going on, be factual as well as inclusive. For example, if you say "As much as we want to help out, the funds would come out of a retirement account we've built so you aren't financially responsible for us later." Not only are you modeling how to navigate challenging situations, but they can also come away with the truth.

When you choose Positive Money, you choose a relationship with money driven by love rather than fear. Therefore, to be financially responsible is an act of love. The following are other ways to think about it through the lens of Positive Money.

- If you want your money to serve a higher good, you might brainstorm different ways to be financially responsible to help make that possible. For example, if a

higher good is safety and security, how are you helping money make that possible?
- If you like the fifth principle of Positive Money being an act of giving and receiving, what does being financially responsible look like through that lens?
- If you endorse the principle of causing no harm, how is your commitment to financial responsibility either creating or reducing harm to yourself or others?

How to:

I recommend starting with the question, "Where am I financially responsible and why?" If you have a simple answer, how can you go deeper? Are you considering all dimensions of money, including earning, spending, saving, and giving? How do you define 'being responsible'? This is where a conversation with money can reveal more information or insights. For instance, if you grew up in a household where money wasn't an issue and you weren't held financially responsible for much, you might still expect others to carry that burden. If you choose a career based on how much money you can make, you might think you're being financially responsible yet spend wildly on non-essentials.

Positive Money can help you with this exercise, especially when you have a practice of mental fitness and can stay focused on what matters most. Here are options for conversations with yourself or others that incorporate Positive Money principles:

- **As a family**, talk about how your money supports a higher good and how each family member can contribute financially or otherwise.
- **As a couple**, explore how choosing Positive Money for each of you changes your relationship to financial responsibilities, if at all.
- **As a parent,** try to model your version of what being financially responsible looks and feels like.

- **As a sibling**, think about how you compare yourself financially to a sibling if at all, and ask yourself if your thoughts cause more harm than good.

Regardless of where you stand in your family system, you likely carry some financial responsibility, even if it's not in all areas of earning, spending, saving, or giving. The question is what that looks and feels like and how Positive Money can help, whether it's deciding who pays for lunch or assisting Mom or Dad's transition to a retirement community. If any of those conversations feel daunting, start with a simple practice of listening and getting curious about a smaller matter with no expectation of resolution. You might be surprised by the outcome.

Siblings and Money

I am one of four sisters and have five children, so I'm familiar with sibling dynamics. As the fourth in line, I remember how important it was to my parents to be fair in their distribution of gifts or money. If I wanted a new pair of skis, they were careful to calibrate how that gift stacked up against those of my siblings. As parents, we've tried to be fair as well though it can be quite the balancing act and create stress around special events like holidays and birthdays.

Though it may seem silly that a price tag can convey anything more than a number, we often measure our worth or how much we're loved by such means. Even if parents do their best to spread their love equally, children don't always see it that way. This is where sibling rivalry and money can get mixed up and even turn ugly.

If you feel yourself in such a place, keep in mind that:

- **It's not about the money.** Positive Money focuses on our relationship with money, not on money itself. If your beef with your sister or brother is over who paid for or got what, or who's more successful based on how much they make, chances are it isn't about the money. More likely, it's about judgment whether it's feeling judged by others or you judging them, yourself, or the circumstance.

- **Each sibling is different.** Regardless of biological or cultural connections, each sibling has a unique and hard-wired way of being in the world. As we discover what this looks like for us, we can get jealous of the qualities we see in a sibling and think less of ourselves as a result.
- **There's no such thing as fair.** In the messy world of familial relationships, there's no such thing as fair or equal. What may seem fair to you may not seem fair to me. *There is no fair fairy.* If you're in a battle to prove something is unfair, you're likely in the wrong battle.

If siblings want to find a way past perceived differences around money, I offer some practices in the next chapter that may help such as Money Dates. Otherwise, the following are optional Positive Money moves according to each principle.

1. **Choose love over fear.** Ask yourself, "What does love look like here?"
2. **Identify the thoughts and beliefs related to money that you bring to the table** and reflect on how they're connected to family dynamics and history.
3. **Focus on the higher good** of repairing the relationship.
4. **Check to see if your head, heart, and habits are aligned** in general, and then specifically in regard to your relationship with money. Note points of misalignment.
5. **Ask what you give and receive now** in your relationship outside of money and how you would like that to change, if at all.

6. **Reflect on how your thoughts, feelings, or actions are causing harm** and where you might see opportunities for mitigating that harm.
7. **What Positive Money practice might you use to try to repair this important relationship?** (Keep in mind that "repair" may look different for different people.)

Couples and Money

I touch on the challenges couples face around money in other parts of the book, so I'll focus here on what you can do to avoid money damaging your relationship.

First, regardless of what drew you together in the first place, you bring equal value to the relationship no matter what's in your bank account. Even if one of you earns significantly more than the other, the qualities you appreciate about one another are your strengths, your values, and your unique qualities. You're building a partnership together. Money is just one resource that helps that structure stand strong.

Second, a relationship needs attention just like a garden, your physical body, or your children. If you don't have a plan for nurturing that relationship, it will wither, no matter what your financial situation.

Third, develop a strategy to talk about money. I offer Money Dates as a way to do this. The more you practice, the easier it will get. Think of it as weeding. If you let the weeds go unattended too long, you have a big job on your hands. If you weed regularly, everyone wins, including the flowers.

---

1. Lieber, Ron. *The Opposite of Spoiled: Raising Kids Who Are Grounded, Generous, and Smart About Money.* New York: HarperCollins, 2015.

Chapter 2

Positive Money Practices

> *At some point, you gotta let go, sit still, and allow contentment to come to you.* - Elizabeth Gilbert

The following Positive Money practices have been effective for my clients and are supported through additional coaching, workshops, and resources available on my website. A key to their success is a regular practice of mental exercises that boost your mental fitness so you can think clearly and make decisions effectively and efficiently. Examples of how to do that follow.

Mental Fitness Exercises

Mental fitness exercises literally change your brain chemistry when you do them consistently and frequently. In this chapter, I give you options for these exercises so you can build your resilience and capacity to do hard things like talking about money. As Viktor Frankl might say, you can't avoid all stimuli, but you can work on managing your reaction by suppressing the impulse to react and choosing a more suitable response instead.

As a reminder, mental fitness is not a replacement for professional care. Rather, it's a way to build the skills and self-awareness so you can more effectively manage your mental health.

How to:

Meditation - There are many forms of meditation practice as well as ways to find support if you are new to it. I use a variety of apps and have taken classes to learn what works for me. A primary goal of meditation is to train your brain to respond to challenges with a greater sense of calm, peace, and balance.

I recommend at least 10-20 minutes of early morning meditation and then short 3-5 minute breaks every few hours throughout the day. An alarm helps as a reminder. The short meditations can consist of closing your eyes, rubbing hands together, or getting up and taking a brief walk.

Breathwork - As we learn more about how our breathing helps us manage stress, we're finding breathwork exercises to be particularly valuable in regulating our response to challenging situations and even reducing our blood pressure. These exercises have been part of yogic practices for centuries and are now being used in corporate and school settings.

I recommend box breathing. Start by sitting upright in a quiet spot.

1. *Slowly exhale out of your mouth, getting all the oxygen out of your lungs.*
2. *Then inhale slowly and deeply through your nose to the count of four. Hold your breath for another slow count of four.*
3. *Then exhale through your mouth for the same slow count of four, expelling the air from your lungs and abdomen.*
4. *Hold your breath for another four seconds. Repeat.*

Money Boundaries

Boundaries are essential to building and maintaining healthy and meaningful relationships. Money boundaries are no exception. They help you clarify needs and limits related to money for yourself and others and can be both internally and externally focused.

Internal boundaries exist in your mind and are emotional, mental, or spiritual. External boundaries live outside your thoughts, feelings, and beliefs and include those that are behavioral, material, physical, sexual, or social.[1]

One of the main reasons we have money challenges in the first place is that we don't set boundaries, know how to manage them, or are unaware of them until we cross them. We know they're important but have little experience in defining them or we're convinced that enforcing them is mean or unreasonable.

For example, fear can stop us from expressing our needs when we expect rejection or a negative reaction from others. These fears can run deep and be associated with experiences where we lacked the skill to respond like being told you must do something far outside your normal work duties and comfort level to earn the raise you asked for.

On the contrary, when you're able to set and maintain boundaries in the spirit of love and kindness toward yourself and others, it can truly transform your relationship with money as well as with food, drink, exercise, etc. For example, if you consistently overspend using credit cards, it would be natural to set a boundary of not using them for a certain period of time. It's not just about the boundary itself, however; it's also about the attitude you have when doing so.

If you set the boundary from a place of fear, you might be afraid that this strategy won't stop your desire to spend or that you'll feel like you're being controlled. If you set the boundary from a place of love, you might get curious about why you desire to spend in the first place and how you might enroll others in your goal without fear of being judged.

I could write a whole book just on setting money boundaries, given the depth of the practice and its opportunity for transformation. For now, the following should help you get started on defining and managing your money boundaries as part of your shift toward Positive Money.

How to:

- **Explore your current understanding and use of boundaries.** Can you think of a money boundary that shapes your relationships with others? If not, can you imagine one that would? Or can you think of a money boundary you've observed in the media? How might clear money boundaries play a role in your emotional, mental, or financial health?
- **If you've set boundaries in the past,** how did you communicate them to others and what went well or could have gone better in managing them?
- **Come up with at least two money boundaries, one internally focused and one externally focused.** (I will practice at least 30 minutes of meditation a day, and only go out to dinner one night a week.) How does it feel to define and set those boundaries? Where are you coming from fear and where are you coming from love?

Money Dates

Money Dates are dedicated times to focus on a money question or challenge either with yourself or others. They are scheduled and have specific intentions like reviewing a budget, talking through a career move, or addressing different ways of money management. The best practice is to start and stop at a pre-designated time, focus on only one topic per date, and make them a routine. It's also advisable to schedule dates at a time when all parties are refreshed and ready to partake in an open-minded discussion.

If there's anything worth investing in, it's a healthy relationship with money in the household or workplace. Money Dates help to achieve that goal. They're most effective when all parties fully engage, communicate with respect, and feel that they're heard and taken seriously. Such involvement fosters collaboration and builds trust. It helps to create a productive atmosphere for your money date, establish agreements ahead of time, and share appreciation.

Sample agreements:

- *I (we) agree that having a healthy relationship with money as a couple or business is well worth the investment of time and energy to define what that means.*
- *I (we) agree that everyone deserves to be heard and has something valuable to bring to the table.*
- *I (we) agree that we want to create a place of psychological safety around a topic that can be rife with conflict and stress, so we commit to listening and learning from one another and having a plan for when we need a break.*

Before my wife and I started Money Dates, I often felt anxious because we didn't have a great track record with money conversations. We would show up with different needs and perspectives and spend more time defending our own rather than understanding those of the other. I wanted to see where our money was going and felt less confident about financial matters. My wife, used to moving money around, is more comfortable with the flow of money. One or both of us would end up in tears or get frustrated with not feeling heard, understood, or appreciated. Though these challenges weren't only about money, they flagged the need for deeper work.

How to:

1. **Schedule one hour of time when you're rested and free of distractions.** If the others you invite to the date back out, then keep the date with yourself. Set an alarm if it helps to keep you on track. I recommend scheduling money dates before or after recurring commitments on your calendar, such as going to church or watching your favorite show. This helps build the habit.
2. **Set clear intentions and goals for the date.** If there are too many topics to discuss, pick one that seems like a priority and assume that you'll need to schedule more Money Dates to cover the others. Start and end on time and be sure to schedule the next one.
3. **Bring chocolate and candles or something else along that represents your rich life.** Take a few minutes before you jump in to appreciate one another or yourself for taking this time and to set some agreements on how you will work together. When done, thank one another for showing up and making the effort even if it feels like you have a way to go until it feels comfortable and productive.

At first, Money Dates can seem stiff or awkward. It's easy to fall off the practice, especially as they may feel challenging. Hang in there! Commit to a schedule and give it a go. Be present, celebrate progress, and focus on what's working. Remember that you appreciate your partner for their strengths and effective teams operate by capitalizing on each member's different strengths. Even if you're birds of a feather, it can be valuable to share what you appreciate about one another as it's easy to get lost in the flock.

If you need more help, no worries. Family and coupled life are the final frontier of the good, the bad, and the ugly of human relationships. It takes time to heal and to trust, and we feel most vulnerable and broken when money is involved. When you come to the table knowing that currency is as much a matter of communication and inquiry as it is about cash, then you can start to find the gifts and opportunities of both knowing *and* not knowing.

Note: I have a guide to money dates on my website.

Money Dialogues

A money dialogue is a conversation you have with money. You talk to money, and it talks back to you. It may sound silly, but it works. I learned this technique from Olivia Mellan, a long-time money coach and author who specialized in money and relationships. It is a simple and powerful way to check in with your relationship with money, whether you have a conversation with yourself or others.

How to:

1. **Pick a quiet place for you and money to have a conversation.** I suggest finding a comfortable chair for yourself and setting up another chair or stool across from you for money. Grab a journal and something to write with.

2. **Once settled, close your eyes and take a few deep breaths.** Scan your body and notice any spots of tension or negative thoughts. Try to let them go.
3. **When ready, turn your focus to money sitting across from you.** Imagine what it would say to you. Try to sit there listening in silence for several minutes before answering these questions: What is it saying to you? What do you want to say to it? Does the exchange motivate you or hold you back?
4. **If you get emotional or frustrated, take a few more breaths to calm your mind and body, and then get curious.** What thoughts and feelings are showing up regarding you or money or both? Are they true? What are the facts? Capture the dialogue as if you were a curious bystander.
5. **As a bonus, think of the Positive Money principle that would bring you closer to money.** How might you work better as a team? What do you both need to make that happen?

Money Maps

Money maps are visual representations of your money activity over a specific period. A traditional money map plots past financial activity for the purposes of building a budget or financial planning. Though a traditional map is useful for getting a reality check on your finances, it can lead to judgments and shame. "I'm sure we spent less than $800 last month on groceries," becomes, "Holy cow, we spent over $1000 on groceries last month!"

Instead, I encourage a "bail on the budget" mentality for this activity, so you get curious about where your money flows and why and start to envision how it can change. The first objective is to notice your thoughts and feelings as you go through the process. The second objective is to get curious about potential blind spots and areas for improvement, no matter how much money is involved.

There are two parts to this activity. The first is to make as many money maps as you want based on memory or perception. The second part is to gather evidence to see how the data compares to your perceptions. You can make companion maps and label them "The Facts," or you can just reflect on the differences you're noticing and the learning you're gaining from the exercise. Remember, this is a creative process. It calls for discernment, not disparagement or blame. If you start to experience shame, take note of those feelings and include them in your drawing if you want.

One reason I like money maps is that they help us find our way, starting with "You are here." If you don't know your location, you look for something that orients you, and sometimes you discover you're in a much different place than you'd thought. For example, I was recently in San Francisco where I hadn't been in over 20 years. I thought it would be fun to visit Yosemite National Park and pictured it on the map. When I actually looked it up, I was surprised by how far off I was. I'm usually good with directions, but clearly, I needed a refresher on California's geography.

Another reason I like this activity is that it sparks the parts of our brain that help us welcome change and innovation. The more maps you make, the better you get at spotting what's missing or out of scale with reality. It may not be clear today, but you'll find your way over time. I like to compare the experience to the discovery that the earth is spherical after ages of assuming it was flat. Such an evidence-based paradigm shift reminds us of the power of inquiry, being open-minded, and having patience with the process.

* * *

At home - Money mapping can be fun for kids and adults. For example, if you ask a 9-year-old to draw a picture of places or things she cares about most, it can prompt a family conversation about values and how people spend time and money differently depending on those values. Her parents could use money maps as a way to deepen an understanding of individual-versus-group needs. If such an intergenerational activity feels challenging, I would remind you that the goal is to learn, not to judge and that the world might still be flat if we didn't challenge assumptions, including our own.

At work - Money mapping can also be a useful tool in the workplace for gauging employees' awareness of their contribution to the company's financial well-being. Too often, they're kept out of the loop of financial decisions or given limited information, so they have no idea of how their daily efforts impact the bottom line. They can get resentful if they see disparities that don't make sense or appear unfair.

How to:

1. **Start with a simple assessment of your money activity *Now* and *In the Past* in four main areas: Earning, Spending, Saving, and Giving.** Try using bubbles or circles to represent the activity over the past year by percentage. For example, your earning bubble might look bigger or smaller than your saving or spending bubbles. *What are you noticing? How are you judging yourself, if at all?*
2. **Once you have one money map, experiment with others.** Maybe you estimate your spending over a specific period and map it to specific categories. You might enlist a partner to do a similar exercise and compare notes. Then look at the actual numbers. Where are the gaps

between your perceptions and the facts? How does your perspective differ from your partners'?

3. **Create a map for future activities.** What might that look like in comparison to the ones you already made? If it's a Positive Money map, how might the principles influence your actions? For example, if you want your money to serve a higher good, what would that look like for your next vacation? If you need to pay off debt, how might you think of that as causing your future self less harm? How might your best self be showing up and a responsible steward of your present resources?

As you do these activities, try to stay as open and curious as possible as it's likely that your demons will want a seat at the table. This is where doing money meditations can help.

Money Meditations

Money meditations are mindful moments throughout your day that focus on a money mantra, affirmation, or question that is top of mind. When you take this time to be present with your thoughts and feelings, you tune in to what matters most and literally build neural pathways that help you engage the thrive-versus-survive parts of your brain. These affirmations and dedicated moments of gratitude support what researchers are finding to be key to our happiness with strong relationships at the top of the list. One Harvard University study determined that it's the robustness of our bonds that most determines whether we feel fulfilled — even more than wealth, I.Q., or social class.[2]

A best practice is to start your day with a longer meditation so you bank the sense of calm and positive affirmation for use throughout the day. Then, every few hours, you stop to give yourself a mental fitness boost by doing mini-meditations for 2-5 minutes that can include closing your eyes and listening intently to sounds around you, getting up and moving around, or rubbing your hands together and noticing the textures of your fingertips.

I include Money Meditations in my list of practices because they've been such a key part of transforming my relationship with money. I've come to accept what I can and can't control, have more empathy toward myself and others, and developed better skills in navigating challenges. I'm also reminded of how these meditations reconnect me to reconnect me the principles of Positive Money.

How to:

1. **Set a timer, as it's easy to forget to pause in your busy day.** You'll want to do this a few times in the morning and afternoon for a total of 20-30 minutes per day. If possible, it's advisable to stack more time in the morning so you can draw on the energy boost later as fatigue sets in.
2. **Settle in with the intention to be as present as possible for 2-5 minutes.** Take a few deep breaths and rub your hands together. If you're sitting, close your eyes if that

feels comfortable. Listen for sounds or smells around you and do a body scan to notice any tightness or resistance. Use your breath to open your airways and bring oxygen into your bloodstream. If your kids are around, invite them to join you.

3. **If you have a money affirmation or mantra, tune into it.** "I'm worthy" or "There's plenty of money" are examples. Repeat the mantra for the duration. Notice without judgment how you feel. If negative or opposing thoughts come up, let them go with kindness and return to your mantra.

Money Stories

Money stories are the tales we tell ourselves about money. They can harken back to our childhood, inform how we choose a career, or determine what we dream about. I've told a number of money stories in this book including mine where the script I've had running in my head, sometimes unconsciously, is that money is bad.

I include this as the last Positive Money practice because it can be one of the most powerful. For example, if you tell yourself you're a fraud, imagine how much harder you'll have to work to make the money you need to thrive.

Change the story, change the outcome.

How to:

1. Take three minutes to write down your thoughts about money.
2. Take one of those thoughts or stories and ask yourself where you learned it.

3. Next, determine what is fact and what is fiction. Fact: I lost my money and got in trouble for it. Fiction: I'm bad with money.
4. Now write a different version of the thought or story. For example, if you tell yourself that you're a fraud and can't change a lot for your services, how might you change that narrative? "I care about this issue and understand what my clients are dealing with. I also know how valuable it can be to work with someone who gets it. I create safe spaces for my clients to transform and that is priceless."

---

1. Source: R1 Learning at https://r1learning.com/
2. Harvard Study of Adult Development at https://www.adultdevelopmentstudy.org/

Chapter 3

Positive Money Support

> *Beware of little expenses. A small leak will sink a great ship.* - Benjamin Franklin

If reading about Positive Money inspires you to snuggle in with your money and figure out how both of you can work together more effectively, you might wonder where and how to get started or what additional support you'll need. In this chapter, I offer an overview of professional services dedicated to financial health and well-being, make recommendations for how to find the tools you need, and introduce an approach to managing your finances that aligns with the principles and practices of Positive Money.

Professional Services

The variety of professional services focused on money can range from practical financial advice and support to behavioral or therapeutic interventions. It's not uncommon to need a little or a lot of both, given how complicated our relationship with money can be. It's also not uncommon to be overwhelmed by the choices, given the range of options, or to resist reaching out because you're embarrassed by your financial situation, habits, or lack of knowledge. On top of all of that, you may have opinions about the services, such as "Financial advisors are only for the wealthy" or "I'm not old enough to need a planner."

Start by asking yourself, "What help do I want or need right now?" Sometimes, it's obvious. Other times, it's hidden behind what you think you want. If you're still not sure, start with what you know and then take the next step, even if it's asking for help.

* * *

Wants versus needs

One of the core lessons in financial education is about differentiating between a want and a need and understanding how each drives our relationship with money in different ways.

- I *want* to have a better marriage. I *need* to set boundaries.
- I *want* to travel to Africa. I *need* a break.
- I *want* to feel more confident about my financial future. I *need* to get out of debt.

It's easy to confuse wants and needs You want a new gadget or pair of shoes when what you really need is a distraction and a dopamine hit. You want a new car when what you really need is reliable transportation. You want more money when what you really need is more flexibility, choice, and freedom.

When the wires get crossed, it's easy to get tripped up. You think you're on the path to a rich life when you're actually taking a detour. For example, you want to feel healthier. Your first thought is to invest in a gym membership. This could be helpful and perhaps a gamechanger. However, without a deeper inquiry into what you really need, you could be missing clues to what got you here in the first place. When you address those needs, you may discover that your wants and expenses change or shift.

When our household was at the height of chaos with two dogs, two cats, five kids, and two working moms, we decided to hire a cleaning service. We wanted a clean house. What we needed was quality time together, less stress around cleaning, and to not feeling embarrassed about the mess when guests came over. We now consider our house cleaning as a form of therapy.

In *The Soul of Money*, Lynne Twist shares her story of having all the wealth to buy what she and her husband thought they wanted – a jet-setting lifestyle, fancy houses, vacations, expensive clothes – until it became clear that what they really needed emotionally and spiritually was to make a difference in the world. This led to big changes in their lifestyle, their relationship with money, and the way they gave and served others. Lynne became an activist and founder of the Pachamama Alliance, a global community driven by the purpose of creating a sustainable future that works for all. Her story is a prime example of the third principle of Positive Money serving a higher good.[1]

* * *

Deciding what you need

If and when you decide you need professional help and reach out to an advisor, planner, coach, or counselor, they will first ask about what you're seeking. You might want financial guidance when what you really need is clarity on goals and priorities or to develop and sustain healthier money habits. Do them (and yourself) a favor by considering your specific goals before your first consultation.

While looking for help, keep in mind that some individuals or firms offer blended services or competencies. For example, I'm a money mindset coach with a counseling background in career and leadership development. Financial planners are often certified as financial advisors. The best strategy is to ask about the scope of services ahead of time and to ask for a free consultation to determine the best fit.

Finally, I advise that you do your due diligence and diversify your assets where possible. It can be tempting to follow the latest trend or to believe in one person who claims to have your back or promises exceptional results. Keep in mind that scamming didn't end with the arrest of Bernie Madoff, the investment advisor who convinced his clients he could consistently deliver high returns when, in fact, he was robbing Peter to pay Paul.

Accountants and Bookkeepers

Accountants and bookkeepers share the same long-term goal of helping you thrive financially in your personal or business life, but they play different roles. Bookkeepers focus on daily responsibilities like recording transactions while accountants provide overarching financial advice and tax guidance. Accountants have a greater responsibility than bookkeepers in that they are accountable for financial records and systems that are in compliance with the law and follow best practices. Accountants also prepare and submit tax returns.

Financial Advisors, Planners, and Educators

Financial advisors and planners specialize in managing money and can range in skill and level of certification. Generally, financial planners help you or your organization create strategies to meet long-term financial goals while advisors serve as brokers, money managers, insurance agents, or bankers.

A gold standard is the Certified Financial Planner or CFP because it requires rigorous education and testing in many areas of financial planning such as retirement, investing, taxes, insurance, and education. CFPs are fiduciaries, meaning that they must act in their client's best interests. It's best to work with a CFP if you're comfortable with finances, looking to build wealth, need life insurance or other products, or are seeking investment advice.

Many CFPs are also registered investment advisors who can advise on investments and manage client assets. Some financial planners and advisors offer fee-only services in that they are not tied to certain products or services they earn commissions on. Be sure to ask about this option when shopping for these services.

Financial educators or financial literacy teachers are more likely found in schools or educational settings where they provide education about money for different ages. I am a certified Financial Educator through the National Financial Educators Council and have developed materials for children and adults under the Pizza Money® brand.

Financial Counselors and Therapists

Financial counselors provide educational and emotional support to help you get on track financially. They're more like a money coach in that they're focused on the future – on helping you get out of debt, set up a budget, manage lines of credit, or prepare for a financial goal like buying a house. The Association for Financial Counseling & Planning Education offers accreditation as a financial counselor, and some of these counselors also become financial fitness coaches where they provide additional coaching and skill-building.

Financial therapists help you understand your current financial behavior by looking at the past. They can specialize in chronic and unhealthy money habits like hoarding, gambling, or similar financial behaviors that can't be resolved through basic coaching or counseling.

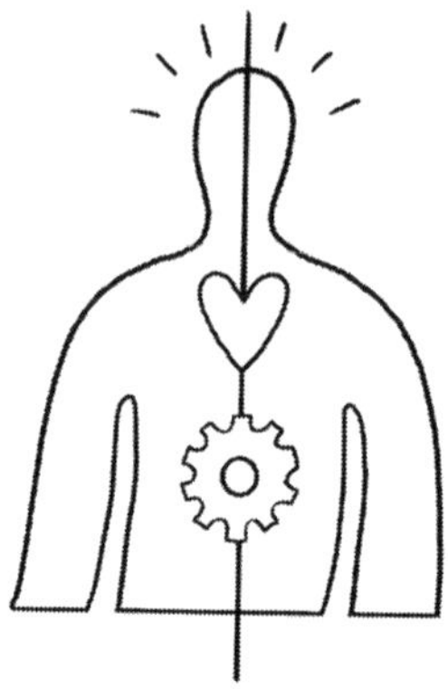

Money Coaches

Coaches generally help you clarify your goals, identify and address obstacles, and improve your performance moving forward, while counselors tend to work with your past to resolve current challenges. Coaches are often trained or certified in a specific approach and may have faced similar challenges. A good coach will ask you powerful questions, keep you focused on a specific objective, and hold you accountable. Some tend toward practical advice and instruction, while others serve as a "guide on the side" as you navigate your own discovery and learning process.

Money coaching is an evolving area of coaching aimed at helping individuals and businesses address financial challenges all across the economic spectrum. Some money coaches have a financial background and work with you much as a financial fitness or counselor would. Other money coaches focus on money mindset and your relationship with money, which is more my area of expertise. Either way, you end up navigating the emotional, behavioral, and practical dimensions of your financial life so you can find greater peace and confidence. If deeper issues arise, it's not uncommon for a coach to refer a client to a therapist or specialist.

* * *

No matter which professional service you choose, it can be one of the best investments you can make given the number of ways your relationship with money drives results around education, career, marriage, or family. Once you find individuals or companies you know, like, and trust, I recommend regular check-ins, whether you think you need them or not, given all the changing circumstances that can affect your financial health and security.

Tools

> *In radio, you have two tools. Sound and silence.* - Ira Glass

What I love about this quote from Ira Glass is that it reminds us of our tendency to overcomplicate things or to lose sight of our purpose. If you're looking for the best tool to manage your personal or business finances or to build your mental fitness, it can be easy to go down the rabbit hole of apps or online software, especially as the marketplace grows at a rapid clip. For example, the growth in digital banking alone is significant. In one study, the global market for online banking was estimated at $12.1 billion in 2020 and is projected to reach $30.1 billion by 2026.[2]

If you're shopping around for a tool, I recommend starting with what you need it for. This may sound obvious, but more often than not, we start by looking for what fits our budget, is recommended by a friend, or makes us feel productive. Not all cooks cook the same and not every tool works for every job. For example, if you asked me for a screwdriver, I would ask for what type of screw. If you asked me to recommend a tool to pay off debt and avoid using credit or debit cards, I might hand you a stack of envelopes for stashing cash for upcoming expenses.

The other advice I give is to look for companies or products that reflect Positive Money principles and practices.

- If you want your money to serve a higher good, how are the companies you choose to buy from doing the same? Are there financial advisors who can help you invest in such companies?
- If you endorse the idea that Positive Money is generational, how might an online tool or app help you and your kids learn about and manage money together?
- If you choose Positive Money, what would it look like to take care of your money so it can take care of you? How about researching banking options or apps that allow you to distribute income into different accounts or allow you to see all of your financial assets in one place?

Let's return to the analogy of a garden. Gardens serve different purposes and needs. If you want your garden to be an ongoing source of food for your family, you plant and tend the garden differently than if you only want to grow flowers in the summer months. Either way, you start with seeds, learn what is needed for the soil and climate, and stick to a routine for maintenance.

---

1. Twist, Lynne. *The Soul of Money: Reclaiming the Wealth of Our Inner Resources.* New York: W.W. Norton & Company, 2003.

2. https://www.businesswire.com/news/home/20211007005508/en/Global-Digital-Banking-Market-Trajectory-Analytics-Report-2021-Market-to-Reach-30.1-Billion-by-2026---Internet-Infrastructure-Provides-the-Cornerstone-for-the-Growth-of-Digital-Banking---ResearchAndMarkets.com

Chapter 4

Positive Money Questions

> *Without wonder and insight, acting is just a trade.*
> *With it, it becomes creation.* - Bette Davis

Throughout this book, I mention the power of questions and their role in your Positive Money practice. The following is a list of questions for each of the 7 Principles that may spark your inquiry and guide your actions at any point you notice the need.

Positive Money is:

1. A choice. *When you choose Positive Money, you choose a relationship with money that's driven by love rather than fear.*

- What does love look like in this situation?
- How is fear weighing in right now?
- What truly matters to me about my relationship with money?

2. Generational. *When you're aware of the beliefs and behaviors you inherit and pass along, you're more intentional about your actions today.*

- Where is my past showing up in a way I find painful, frustrating, or otherwise objectionable?
- What am I doing today that will have a negative or positive impact on the next generation, and why should I care?
- How might I shift my thinking to lead me toward a different outcome?

3. Serves a higher good. *When you're grounded by a higher good, you have the interests and needs of others in mind.*

- What is my greatest goal here?
- How is my relationship with money connected to what I care about most?
- Where am I inspired to be my greatest self?

4. Aligns head, heart, and habit. *When your thoughts, feelings, and actions related to money are aligned, you experience ease and flow.*

- Where am I feeling out of alignment and why?
- What thoughts are driving my actions in this situation and how do they align or not align with what matters most?
- How do my thoughts, feelings, or actions need to change if I want a different outcome?

5. **An act of giving and receiving.** *When you give and receive equally, you experience the power of connection.*

- Where do I give but not receive easily or vice versa?
- What are the thoughts that help or hinder the give-and-receive muscles?
- How might practicing more of this principle enrich my life?

6. Causes no harm. *When you understand how your money choices cause harm to yourself and others, you take action to mitigate that harm.*

- How might this transaction or interaction with money be causing harm to myself or others?
- Where can I reduce the harm in my relationship with money?
- What would my relationship with money look like if I didn't beat myself up about it so much?

7. A practice. *When you practice Positive Money, you apply the principles to daily financial decisions with mindfulness and compassion.*

- What stops me from being mindful of my money?
- Where can I practice more compassion in my relationship with money?
- How do I currently approach financial decisions, and what would it look like to be more mindful or compassionate toward yourself or others?

Chapter 5

A Call to Action

> *Every day brings new choices.* - Martha Beck

If the idea of Positive Money resonates and you're inspired to bring more of it into your life, congratulations! If you've read through the book this far, you're well on your way. The next step is to make some Positive Money moves.

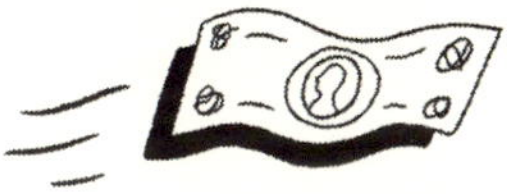

- **Switch it up.** Think about your life in the next 24 hours. Where can you anticipate an interaction with money? How might you switch it up by applying a Positive Money principle? If you can't think of a specific opportunity, create one.

- **Company values.** Think of one of your favorite products to buy. Do you know the company's values? If not, take five minutes to see if you can find their values listed on their website or otherwise. How serious are they about living those values? How important is it that you know, like, and trust them? What would it feel like to support a company more aligned with what you can about?

- **Reframe a thought.** Think of one negative thought about money that you carry around. How do you feel when you think that thought? Now reframe the thought and notice the change in how you feel. (Example: "I'm bad with money" becomes "I care about money.") In the process of reframing, notice the assumptions you make and the opportunities for learning more without judgment.
- **Reach out to a long-lost friend.** A rich life is fed by meaningful connections. Think about a friend you've lost touch with and reach out and send them a letter, call them up, or schedule a visit. Ask yourself what's stopping you if you resist. If you think it's a waste of time for you or the other person, think back on the priceless moments of friendship and who or where you would be without them today.
- **Have a conversation with money.** Find ten minutes to sit down and have a conversation with money. (I describe Money Dialogues in the previous pages.) What did you say to it? What does it say back? What does it need to know to be a more powerful resource in your life? What do you need to believe and do for that to be so?
- **Access the exclusive book bonuses** at www.positivemoneyclub.com by using your book order confirmation number. You'll find more information about emotions, values, and other valuable resources to support your Positive Money journey.

* * *

As you take an action, take a moment to commend yourself. Positive reinforcement works! If you take just one small Positive Money step every day or think of it as progress over perfection, imagine where you can be in a week, six months, or a year from now.

Whatever that looks like, may it be purposeful, practiced, and positive.

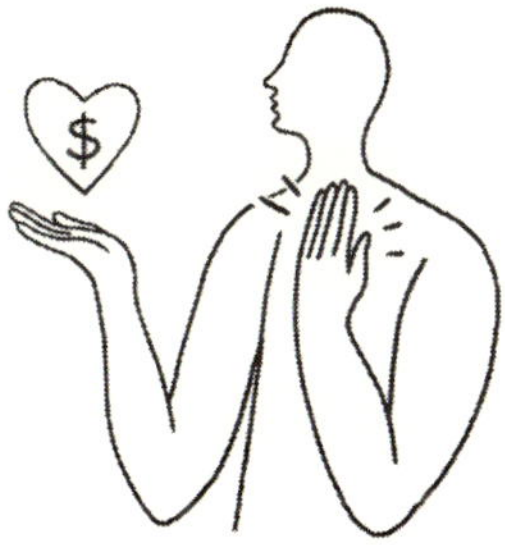

Thank you for being on this journey with me and may we continue on this path together. — CMJ

About the Author

Cindy Morgan-Jaffe, M.Ed., NCC, PRC, CPRC, CPQC helps her clients move beyond the shame, resistance, and fear many have around money so they can live productive and balanced lives. She brings her creativity, passion, and experience to the table with over twenty-five years of work with individuals and teams to enhance performance, develop mental and financial fitness, and build confidence in an area of life that can often feel overwhelming and stressful.

In addition to her professional training and experience, Cindy draws from her 60+ years of navigating life as a sibling, parent, partner, friend, and human. She lives with her wife and pets in Washington, DC, and enjoys hiking and yoga, art, and learning.

Credentials:

- *Nationally Certified Counselor*
- *Certified Positive Intelligence® Coach*
- *Certified XChange Guide and Facilitator*

- *Certified money and life coach who has worked in career, talent, and leadership development in the private, nonprofit, and government sectors*
- *Certified Financial Educator through the National Financial Educators Council*
- *Certified Professional Recovery Coach through the International Institute of Recovery Coaches and International Center for Addiction and Recovery Education*
- *Master's in Education and Human Development from George Washington University with a focus on school counseling and career development for youth*

* * *

Cindy can be reached at:

Website: www.positivemoneyclub.com

Linked In: https://www.linkedin.com/in/morganjaffe/

Instagram: https://www.instagram.com/positivemoneyclub/

Acknowledgments

I want to thank all who have helped make this book possible. To my wife Tanya, you are my rock. To our children Anna, Rose, Claire, Paul, and Olivia, you bring me joy every day. To my sisters Wendy, Kaidi, Penny, and Lisa, you've taught me so much. To Mom and Dad, thank you for all you made possible.

I also want to thank my daughter Rose for her illustrations, my book coach Debra for her guidance and belief in this project, and my editor Ryan for his thoughtful questions. To Meadow, thank you for introducing me to this work. To my accountability buddies and manuscript readers — you know who you are — thank you for your sage guidance and wisdom.

Finally, I want to thank my elder, wiser self who kept cheering me on even when I was ready to give up.

Bibliography

Adams, Ph.D., Marilee. *Change Your Questions, Change Your Life.* Oakland, CA: Berrett-Koehler, 2015.

Adams, Ph.D., Marilee. *The Art of the Question: A Guide to Short-term QUestion-Centered Therapy.* John Wiley & Sons, 1998.

Beck, Martha. *The Way of Integrity*: Finding the Path to Your True Self. London: Little Brown, 2021.

Barrett, Lisa Feldman Barrett. *How Emotions are Made: The Secret Life of the Brain.* Boston: Houghton Mifflin Harcourt, 2018.

Bateson, Mary Catherine. *Composing a Life.* New York: Penguin Group, 1990.

Boc, Victor. *How to Solve All Your Money Problems Forever: Creating a Positive Flow of Money into Your Life.* Berkley Publishing Group, 2013.

Bissonnette, Zac. *How to be Richer, Smarter, and Better-Looking Than Your Parents.* New York: Penguin Group, 2012.

Bradberry, Travis, and Greaves, Jean. *Emotional Intelligence 2.0.* Sandiego, CA: TalentSmart, 2009.

Bridges, Ph.D., William, and Susan Bridges. *Managing Transitions: Making the Most of Change.* Hachette Book Group, 2016.

Brown, Ph.D., LSW, Brené. *Atlas of the Heart: Mapping Meaningful Connection and the Language of Human Experience.* First Edition. New York: Random House, 2021.

Brown, Ph.D., LSW, Brené. *Braving the Wilderness: The Quest for True Belonging and the Courage to Stand Alone.* New York: Random House, 2017.

Brown, Ph.D., LSW, Brené. *The Gifts of Imperfection.* Center City, MN: Hazelden, 2010.

Clear, James. *Atomic Habits: An Easy & Proven Way to Build Good Habits & Break Bad Ones.* New York: Penguin Random House, 2018.

Chamine, Shirzad. *Positive Intelligence.* Austin, Texas: Greenleaf Book Group, 2012.

Chatsky, Jean and Roizen, Michael F. Roizen. *Age Proof: Living Longer Without Running Out of Money or Breaking a Hip.* New York: Hatchett Book Group, 2017.

Chatsky, Jean. *Money Rules: The Simple Path to Lifelong Security.* New York: Rodale, 2012.

Denise Duffield-Thomas. *Chill and Prosper: The New Way to Grow Your Business, Make Millions, and Change the World.* Carlsbad, California: Hay House, 2022.

Devor, Meadow. *Money Love: A Guide to Changing the Way You Think About Money.* United States, 2011.

Dweck, Ph.D., Carol S. *Mindset: The New Psychology of Success.* New York: Ballantine Books, 2008.

Edmondson, Amy C. *The Fearless Organization: Creating Psychological Safety in the Workplace for Learning, Innovation, and Growth.* New Jersey: John Wiley & Sons, 2019.

Fogg, Ph.D., B.J. *Tiny Habits: Small Changes That Change Everything.* Houghton Mifflin Harcourt, 2020.

Frankl, Viktor. *Man's Search for Meaning: An Introduction to Logotherapy.* Boston, Beacon Press, 1992.

Friedland, MD, Daniel. *Leading Well from Within: A Neuroscience and Mindfulness-Based Framework for Conscious Leadership.* San Diego, CA: SuperSmartHealth, 2016.

Gikandi, David Cameron. *A Happy Pocket Full of Money: Infinite Wealth and Abundance in the Here and Now.* Charlottesville, VA: Hampton Roads Publishing, 2011.

Gilbert, Daniel. *Stumbling on Happiness.* New York: Random House, 2006.

Golman, Daniel. *Emotional Intelligence: Why it can matter more than IQ.* New York: Bantam Books, 1995.

Golman, Daniel. Focus: *The Hidden Driver of Excellence.* New York: HaperCollins, 2013.

Hicks, Esther and Jerry, the Teachings of Abraham. *Money, and the Law of Attraction.* Carlsbad, California: Hay House, 2008.

Katie, Byron. *Loving What Is: Four questions that can change your life.* New York: Three Rivers Press, 2002.

Kaufman, Sarah L. *The Art of Grace: On Moving Well Through Life.* New York: W.W. Norton & Company, 2016.

Kennedy, Dan S. *No B.S. Wealth Attraction in the New Economy.* Entrepreneur Press, 2010.

Kiyosaki, Robert. *Rich Kid Smart Kid: Giving Your Child a Financial Head Start.* New York: Warner Books, 2001.

Klontz, Brad, Psy.D and Klontz, Ted, Ph.D. and Kahler, Rick, CFP. *Wired for Wealth.* Deerfield Beach, Florida: Health Communications, 2008.

Kobliner, Beth. *Make Your Kid a Money Genius Even If You're Not.* New York: Simon & Schuster, 2017.

Kotter, John P. *Change: How Organizations Achieve Hard-to-Imagine Results in Uncertain and Volatile Times.* New Jersey: John Wiley & Sons, 2021.

Kruger, David, M.D. with Mann, John David. *The Secret Language of Money.* New York: McGraw Hill, 2009

Lally, Tammy. *Money Detox.* Florida: Little Lindsey Press, 2018.

Lieber, Ron. *The Opposite of Spoiled: Raising Kids Who Are Grounded, Generous, and Smart About Money.* New York: HarperCollins, 2015.

Mellan, Olivia with Christie, Sherry. *The Advisor's Guide to Money Psychology.* New Jersey: Investment Advisor Press, 2004.

Mellan, Olivia with Christie, Sherry. *Overcoming Overspending.* Washington, DC: Money Harmony Books, 2009.

Michalowicz, Mike. *Profit First.* New York: Random House, 2017.

Mundis, Jerrold. *Making Peace With Money.* Kansas City, MO: Andrews McMeel, 1999.

Mundis, Jerrold. *How to Have More Money.* 2012.

Nemeth, Ph.D., Maria. *The Energy of Money: A Spiritual Guide to Financial and Personal Fulfillment.* New York: Random House, 2000.

Northrup, Kate. *Money, A Love Story.* Carlsbad, CA: Hay House, 2013.

Olen, Helaine. *Pound Foolish: Exposing the Dark Side of the Personal Finance Industry.* New York: Penguin Group, 2013.

Olen, Helaine, and Pollack, Harold. *The Index Card: Why Personal Finance Doesn't Have to be Complicated.* New York: Penguin Group, 2017.

Patterson, Kerry, Grenny, Joseph, McMillan, and Switzler, Al. *Crucial Conversations.* McGraw-Hill, 2012.

Price, Debra. *Money Therapy.* Novato, CA: New World Library, 2000.

Price, Debra. *Money Magic: Unleashing Your True Potential for Prosperity and Fulfillment.* Novato, CA: New World Library, 2000.

Prochaska, Ph.D., James O. *Changing to Thrive: Using the Stages of Change to Overcome the Top Threats to Your Health and Happiness.* Center City, MN: Hazelden Publishing, 2016.

Ramsey, Dave. *The Total Money Makeover: A Proven Plan for Financial Fitness.* Nashville, TN: Nelson Books, 2013.

Ramsey, Dave. *Financial Peace Revisited.* New York: Penguin Group, 2003.

Roth, Geneen. *Lost and Found: Unexpected Revelations About Food and Money.* New York: Penguin Group, 2011.

Seligman, Martin E.P. *Flourish: A Visionary New Understanding of Happiness and Well-Being.* New York: Free Press, 2011.

Singletary, Michelle. *The 21-Day Financial Fast.* Grand Rapids, MI: Zondervann, 2013.

Singer, Michael A. *The Untethered Soul: The Journey Beyond Yourself.* Oakland, CA: New Harbinger, 2007.

Sisodia, Raj and Mackey, John. *Conscious Capitalism: Liberating the Heroic Spirit of Business.* Boston: Harvard Business School Publishing Corporation, 2014.

Sisodia, Raj and Gelb, Michael J. *The Healing Organization: Awakening the Conscience of Business to Help Save the World.* HarperCollins, 2019.

Smith, Margaret H. Smith, Ph.D. *Money: From Fear to Love.* Ennea Coaching, 2011.

Stanney, Barbara Stanny. *Secrets of Six-Figure Women.* New York: HarperCollins, 2002.

Stanney, Barbara Stanny. *Overcoming Underearning.* New York: HarperCollins, 2005.

Stavros, Jackie, and Torres, Cheri. *Conversations Worth Having: Using Appreciative Inquiry to Fuel Productive and Meaningful Engagement.* Oakland, CA: Berrett-Koehler Publishers, 2022.

Stixrud, William, Ph.D. and Johnson, Ned. *The Self-Driven Child: The Science and Sense of Giving Your Kids More Control Over Their Lives.* Penguin Books, 2019.

The Arbinger Institute. *The Anatomy of Peace: Resolving the Heart of Conflict.* Oakland, CA: Berret-Koehler, 2015.

Bibliography

The Arbinger Institute. *The Outward Mindset: Seeing Beyond Ourselves.* Oakland, CA: Berret-Koehler, 2016.

Twist, Lynne. *The Soul of Money: Reclaiming the Wealth of Our Inner Resources.* New York: W.W. Norton & Company, 2003.

Warren, Elizabeth and Warren Tyagi, Amelia. *All Your Worth: The Ultimate Lifetime Money Plan.* New York: Simon & Shuster, 2005.

Winget, Larry. *You're Broke Because You Want to Be.* New York: Penguin Group, 2008.

Wolf, Pd.D., Anthony E. *Get Out of My Life but First Could You Drive Me and Cheryl to the Mall?* HarperCollins, 1991.

Whitehead, Bert, MBD, JD. *Why Smart People Do Stupid Things with Money: Overcoming Financial Dysfunction.* Dexter, Michigan: Thomson-Shore, 2018.

Made in the USA
Middletown, DE
15 March 2023

26846734R00116